'The deepest questions in life – about cha[...]
comfort, and above all hope – cannot be answered by any technical
solution. They ultimately require finding and meeting personally the
God whose peace is "beyond our understanding". In this personal, deep
and practical book, Roger Carswell gives us a magnificent glimpse of
how faith in Christ makes a real difference in a messed-up world. I
warmly recommend it to anyone, but especially to those who feel
"weary and burdened".'

Pablo Martinez, psychiatrist and writer

'Where is God? Where he has always been and always will be – in
control! Roger skilfully leads us to realize that the agonized "why?" can
be swallowed up in greater peace, as we thank God for trusting us
through the suffering rather than delivering us from it.'

Helen Roseveare, doctor captured by Simba rebels during the Congo uprising

'Roger's response [to the question of suffering] is biblical, thoughtful,
sensitive and compassionate. I have benefited greatly from reading this
book, and will certainly always have copies to give to people with
questions.'

Justin Mote, church minister

'What makes Roger's book so powerful is his ability to bring together a
wide array of Bible verses with real-life examples which speak to the lives
of Christians today. Roger doesn't shy away from the difficult subject of
suffering, but provides a realistic and compassionate view of how
Christians can respond when faced with it.'

Gordon Corera, BBC correspondent

'Every time I buy a copy of this book I end up giving it away and buying
another! That says something about the value of a book with such a bold
title. The book reaches both heart and mind and gives hope without
being clichéd and simplistic. Buy two, and make sure you give one away!'

Sheila Stephen, counsellor and lecturer

Living with questions
Looking for answers

ivp

WHERE IS GOD

IN A MESSED UP

WORLD

?

ROGER
CARSWELL

INTER-VARSITY PRESS
Norton Street, Nottingham NG7 3HR, England
Email: ivp@ivpbooks.com
Website: www.ivpbooks.com

First published 2006. This edition 2009.

British Library Cataloguing-in-Publication Data
A catalogue record for this book is available from the British Library.

ISBN: 978-1-84474-353-7

Set in Dante 12/15pt
Typeset in Great Britain by CRB Associates, Reepham, Norfolk
Printed and bound by Ashford Colour Press Ltd, Gosport, Hampshire

Inter-Varsity Press publishes Christian books that are true to the Bible
and that communicate the gospel, develop discipleship and strengthen the
church for its mission in the world.

Inter-Varsity Press is closely linked with the Universities and Colleges
Christian Fellowship, a student movement connecting Christian Unions
in universities and colleges throughout Great Britain, and a member
movement of the International Fellowship of Evangelical Students.
Website: www.uccf.org.uk

This book is for
Barbara and
John Hill

You have allowed me to suffer much hardship,
    but you will restore me to life again
    and lift me up from the depths of the earth.
You will restore me to even greater honour
    and comfort me once again.
(Psalm 71:20–21 NLT)

CONTENTS

ACKNOWLEDGMENTS

Grateful thanks to my wife and friend, Dot, who has demonstrated on a daily basis the strength and confidence that God gives in the face of injustice, suffering, pain and family struggles. I love her, admire her and thank God for her.

Thanks also to friends who have shared their own personal struggles and helped to keep a human, personal perspective when considering the issue of suffering.

I learned much from my travels to the Middle East, India and, more recently, Nicaragua. The dire poverty and sense of injustice, particularly when compared to the wealth and indulgence I have witnessed in Europe and the USA, have greatly disturbed me.

While I have not suffered to the extent of many, a dark period of depression took me to the depths, and I thank God for all he taught me during this time. His Word, the Bible, has been my instructor and source of help over many years.

I am also grateful to the hundreds of individuals with whom I have discussed and debated the issues covered in this book. Their genuine questions provided the basis for the book.

Finally, my thanks to IVP, and particularly to my editors: Emma Balch, who has used her skills to improve immensely what appears in this book, and Eleanor Trotter, for her encouragement and patience in getting this book to where it is today.

PREFACE

I first witnessed a shanty town when I was thirteen. Having been brought up in England, nothing could have prepared me for the shock of seeing such dire poverty and destitution in the Middle East.

Years later the memory of that first shock gripped me again while I was working in India and Nicaragua. I was deeply stirred by the empty faces and staring eyes of those living off the scraps they found in rubbish tips, trying to get to anything edible before the dogs and birds beat them to it. A week before I arrived in Nicaragua, in the town next to where I was working, eleven people were discovered in one house, having starved to death. It left me very sombre throughout my time there. I listened eagerly as locals explained the socio-economic injustices that led to such situations. I felt the shame of belonging to a part of the world which exploits other parts for its own self-interest.

I would love to make poverty history. I long for the day when suffering and tears are banished for ever. As an ordinary human being, I feel something of the hurt and pain of those who really do experience suffering. I have wrestled with issues as to why, and this little book is an attempt to answer these big questions. I am just as certain that there is a God who creates and cares, as I am that this world is not as God designed it.

Roger Carswell, January 2006

INTRODUCTION

The Student Union bar is packed. Chairs, sofas and floor space are taken up, and it's standing room only. Students tuck into baked potatoes and listen intently. The floor is opened up and they start firing questions.

'I stopped believing in God when my best friend was killed last year. You say God is loving, but if that's true, why would he allow that to happen?'

'What was the point in praying to God about my dad's cancer if he was going to let him die anyway?'

'If God is so powerful, why couldn't he stop a tsunami from happening?'

'If there is a God, then he must be a malicious one, to send disasters and diseases like earthquakes and AIDS. Is he enjoying punishing us?'

[From a medical student] 'When every day I see people ill and
suffering and some dying, I just can't believe there's a God who
is relevant to this life at all.'

I spend a lot of time visiting universities and colleges, and
everywhere I go I meet students who make these points
and ask these kinds of questions. For many young people,
their life experience to date hasn't brought much personal
tragedy. Meet older generations, and they have the same
questions, but often weighed down with heaviness of heart
or a sense of despair at the state of the world. The subject of
suffering – and, more specifically, why God doesn't stop
wars, pain, death, tragedy and disaster – is without doubt
the issue people struggle with when it comes to Christianity.
I can understand why.

I have given my life to sharing with others the truth about
Jesus Christ and the hope he brings. I believe it to be
absolutely true. However, at times I have to admit that I too
battle with reconciling this message with the reality of the
world around us. I am deeply distressed when I hear of
hundreds killed in a train crash in north India, a baby born
with a serious disability, two beautiful little girls murdered at
the hands of a school caretaker, terrorist bombs exploding on
crowded tubes or buses in London, or the death of my close
friend's son at the age of ten.

I don't have an answer for all the 'whys' that I ask and that
people often ask me. But I do have total confidence in the
character of God and his words to humankind as expressed
in the Bible. I have studied what the Bible says about God,
and I have seen his transforming power in my life and the
lives of others. As a result, I am convinced that we do have
an explanation for why the world is as it is and why God
doesn't put an immediate end to all that is wrong with the

world. I am also convinced that we can find comfort and hope in him. Christians don't have to be silent on the subject of suffering.

The first section of this book looks the reality of suffering squarely in the face and poses the question, 'Why does suffering exist?' It considers some of the reasons behind our questions about suffering, the places we search for answers, and whether we can ultimately find the responses we are looking for.

The second section focuses on what Christians believe about why the world is in the dire state that it is in. It explains how God intended the world to be, what has gone wrong, and what he has done – and is doing – about it. The challenge here is to work out whether what the Bible says is true. Are Christians deluded, or not? Is Christianity worth further investigation? Can you share the same certainty as Christians that God *is* in control and isn't silent?

The third section of the book considers how the Christian faith can help us deal with pain, avoid bitterness and find comfort, and even discover benefits out of tragedy. Each of the chapters in this section is followed by a case study. These personal stories are there to provide examples of people in different circumstances who have found God in a messed-up world. Right at the end of the book, in Appendix I, are some verses from the Psalms. These are good to turn to in times of trouble.

You may be very sceptical about God and how he can speak into all that's wrong with the world. I am also aware that your reason for picking up this book may be because you are carrying deep hurt and raw pain. Please forgive me if at any point I sound glib. It's tough to write generally on a subject which is often deeply personal. I don't claim to be an expert, but I am sure that you can find hope, certainty and answers.

Part One

Searching for God in a
messed-up world

A universal paradox

John Diamond, Jean-Dominique Bauby and Ivan Noble are all now famed for writing about their struggle with terminal illness. John Diamond was working as a journalist for *The Times* when he was diagnosed with throat cancer. He eloquently described his journey towards death in a weekly column for the paper. Jean-Dominique Bauby, previously editor-in-chief of the French magazine *Elle*, was paralysed from a stroke. His autobiographical account, *The Diving-Bell and the Butterfly*, which was dictated by 'blinking', captures his claustrophobic struggle with paralysis. It sold over 150,000 copies in the first week of publication. More recently, the young BBC journalist Ivan Noble chronicled his battle with terminal cancer on the BBC website, a story which is now published in book form under the title *Like a Hole in the Head*.

Surely following the final journal of a dying man is somewhat strange, a little too voyeuristic? The flood of comments received by the BBC when Noble announced he was too ill to continue the online journal suggests otherwise. People from around the globe sent in their words of appreciation. Many had read each journal entry submitted over three years and thanked Noble for giving them perspective, hope, comfort and inspiration. They were moved by his story of courage, and it had made them determined to make more of life or to cope with their own suffering.

Similarly, *The Diving-Bell and the Butterfly* has inspired thousands of readers to appreciate the tragedies (diving bell) and the joys (butterfly) of life. Perhaps the popularity of his book is due to Bauby's success in capturing the paradox we each live with on a daily basis. Not all of us can relate to the deep pain of personal tragedy, but we do see and read news of natural disasters, conflict, poverty, suffering and tragic loss of life. We have all experienced some form of disappointment, injustice, pain or tragedy; yet we also have things to celebrate, things that amaze us, catch us by surprise, warm our heart or put a smile on our face. Sometimes it is the very thing that hurts us which also causes us to experience joy. Certainly, from his hospital bed, Bauby appreciated anew the wonder of life that most of us take for granted – alphabet letters, the taste of 'a simple soft-boiled egg with fingers of toast and lightly salted butter', and the sound of 'blessed silence'.[1]

This tension between the good and the bad, the things we celebrate and those we mourn, is a universal experience. No place or culture on earth is free from it. Young people die in remote communities in Tibet in the same way as they do in Mexico City; train crashes have killed people in India just as they have in Japan; children have been murdered indiscriminately in Tasmania and in Scotland; thousands have been victims of massive natural disasters from Indonesia to the USA.

Asking the question, 'Why?'

Behind the question, 'Where is God in a messed-up world?' is the question 'Why?' – Why is the world in the mess it is in? Why can't God do something about it, if indeed he *really* exists? The media are constantly feeding us with images and stories that fuel this question. One in five of the world's population lives in extreme poverty. Ten million children a year die before their fifth birthday, mostly from preventable diseases. The twenty-year conflict in Sudan has caused over two million deaths and resulted in around four million displaced people and widespread famine. The natural response to statistics like these is 'Why?'

On 26 December 2004 a massive earthquake ripped apart the seabed off the coast of Sumatra, causing the world's worst ever tsunami. It claimed over 150,000 lives and had devastating effects in Indonesia, the Maldives, India, Sri Lanka and Somalia among others. The impact of such a huge tragedy – both immediate and long term – is hard to comprehend. Again it begs the question, 'Why?'

Hardly hitting the headlines, due to the extensive world-wide coverage of the tsunami, the Argentine capital of Buenos Aires faced a tragedy of its own at the close of 2004. Almost 200 young people were killed in a fire that swept through a nightclub in a poor district of the city on 30 December. The death toll almost seemed insignificant in comparison to the tens of thousands being reported dead in Asia the same week, but demonstrations in the streets of Buenos Aires were fuelled by the same question: 'Why?'

No-one is immune

For those of us who have not experienced tragedy on a personal level, however, we can remain complacent, watching and hearing of war and disaster far from home. We are privileged enough to have confidence in our health services, or at least our emergency services, to rescue us, and we are fairly optimistic that we will be accident or disease free. We can feel emotion when we see images of children dying of starvation, but we then turn off the TV and tuck into a curry.

The North American novelist and playwright Thornton Wilder cut into such smugness in his book *The Bridge of San Luis Rey*. In this deceptively simple story he unwraps the complex thoughts of those who narrowly missed death in a tragic accident. On 20 July 1714, Wilder explains, 'the finest bridge in all Peru' collapsed. Five travellers plunged to their death, causing all those who had previously crossed the bridge to question their evidently misplaced confidence:

> The bridge seemed to be among the things that would last forever; it was unthinkable that it should break. The moment a Peruvian heard of the accident he signed himself [with the cross] and made a mental calculation as to how recently he had crossed by it and how soon he had intended crossing by it again. People wandered about in a trance-like state, muttering: they had the hallucination of seeing themselves falling into a gulf.[2]

Whether we are victims or perpetrators, everyone is affected by injustice, evil, disease, disaster or death. Suffering is inescapable. In ancient times, Job, whose story is featured in the Bible, mused that just as sparks fly if two flints are hit together, so human beings eventually suffer. Death comes to all, but so does sadness, heartache and pain. We can avoid struggle and confrontation for a while, but eventually it affects us all.

An ancient question
Although the question 'Why?' is substantial, it is not new. It is raised in the book of Job, the oldest book within the Bible.

The protagonist, Job, lost everything in a matter of days. His sons and daughters were killed, his business collapsed and he lost his health. He asked, 'Why?' And who can blame him? He desperately sought answers, not always in the right places, but he wanted to understand his own predicament. Years later one of the Bible's most powerful preachers, Habakkuk, asked God the same question when his country was being invaded by the barbarous Babylonians. Although he accepted that his people had been far from virtuous, Habakkuk couldn't understand how things would be better under the rule of a nation which was notorious for its torturous and wicked ways.

The Bible has many heroes and some great characters, but its focal person is Jesus. It anticipates his coming to earth, then describes his life and work, his death and resurrection, before applying the effect of his accomplishments to a fledgling church and to Christian believers of all time. Yet Jesus has been described as the 'suffering servant'; God himself identifies with the sorrows and heartache of the world. For two thousand years those who have

The biblical writers were no strangers to the painful effects of suffering.

trusted and followed Jesus have been a people who have suffered through persecution, poverty and derision, as well as through the ordinary trials of life.

Using images and pictures to convey the depth of their hurt, various Bible authors describe in distilled emotion the trials they experienced. It is like being in a furnace,[3] or in a storm,[4] or in warfare,[5] or like experiencing travail and giving birth,[6] or being threshed after harvest,[7] or running a race,[8] or enduring a judicial trial.[9] The biblical writers were no strangers to the painful effects of suffering.

Attempts to provide answers to the question 'Why?' are many, but few are satisfactory. After all, if there is a God and we are part of his creation, who are we to understand his ways? If God is God, then surely he can do as he wishes. He is always going to be beyond our comprehension. We read in the Bible that God says, 'For my thoughts are not your thoughts, neither are your ways my ways.'[10] On the other hand, surely it is right to use the enquiring mind that God has given us to search out and wrestle with issues such as these: 'Where is God in a messed-up world?' 'Why doesn't he stop the injustice, wars and poverty in the world?' 'If he doesn't intervene, is he really a God of love?' 'What is the meaning of *my* suffering?'

2. LOOKING FOR ANSWERS

Two realities

> Never shall I forget that night, the first night in camp, which has
> turned my life into one long night, seven times cursed and seven
> times sealed. Never shall I forget that smoke. Never shall I forget
> the little faces of the children, whose bodies I saw turned into
> wreaths of smoke beneath a silent blue sky.
>
> Never shall I forget those flames which consumed my faith
> forever.
>
> Never shall I forget that nocturnal silence which deprived me,
> for all eternity, of the desire to live. Never shall I forget those
> moments, which murdered my God and my soul and turned my
> dreams to dust. Never shall I forget these things, even if I am
> condemned to live as long as God himself. Never.[1]

These words were penned by Nobel Peace Prize winner Elie
Wiesel, describing his first night of captivity at Auschwitz

concentration camp. He was born to a Jewish family in Sighet, Transylvania, in 1928. Both his parents and his younger sister were killed in the extermination camps, but he survived and later became Professor in Humanities and University Professor at Boston University, as well as a prolific writer.

The writings of Elie Wiesel are powerful prose, but there is intrigue too. Wiesel combines his certainty that God is real with a temporary loss of faith because of the horrendous suffering he witnessed. Later in life, as a Jew, he wrote with confidence about his belief in God. I can relate to Wiesel's sentiments. I have not experienced suffering like he did as a young boy, but I do wrestle with the two realities of God being God and the world being as it is.

Wanting it both ways

Whether we like to admit it or not, our world is character-ized by suffering and evil. Sometimes it seems as though the whole earth is rotten to the core. Even within ourselves we see that there is something like a seed that grows within us and permeates every part of our being, leading us to do wrong. However, we recognize that we should not be like this. It is not that God is playing games with us. We have turned our backs on God and his ways, and inevitably suffer the consequences. Some of us want to know God, but we all want to do our own thing. We don't like God to control us, but we would prefer to live without suffering the consequence of a world in rebellion against him.

However much we may marginalize God, we still want him to be accountable to standards of what we believe to be fair, just, loving and helpful to us. So when trouble strikes we ask, 'Why doesn't God act in a decisive way?' 'Where is he in the maze of human existence?' The Greek philosopher Epicurus outlined the dilemma facing the thinking mind:

> God either wishes to take away evils and is unable; or he is able and is unwilling; or he is neither willing nor able; or he is both willing and able. If he is willing but unable, he is feeble, which is not in accordance with the character of God. If he is able and unwilling, he is envious, which is equally at variance with God. If he is neither willing nor able, he is both envious and feeble, and therefore not God. If he is both willing and able, which alone is suitable for God, from what source then are evils? Or why does he not remove them?[2]

Two millennia later, the English novelist and poet Thomas Hardy found himself facing similar questions. In the unsatisfactory state of having basic, unanswered questions, but fearing that God is either impotent or cruel, he wrote the poem 'Nature's Questioning':

> We wonder, ever wonder, why we find us here!
>
> Has some Vast Imbecility,
> Mighty to build and blend,
> But impotent to tend,
> Framed us in jest, and left us now to hazardry?[3]

A spiritual dimension

There is within every human being an awareness of something 'Other'. There is a spiritual dimension, an incurably religious bent deep inside the psyche of us all. This consciousness of something or someone greater than ourselves leads us to pray, to ask bewildering questions, or to blame someone other than ourselves. Others simply dismiss belief in

God, but in doing so confine themselves to the belief that life is a meaningless cul-de-sac. They take a giant 'step of faith' in saying that there is no designer behind the design, no maker behind the things made and no creator behind creation. Though Richard Dawkins and Jacques Derrida argue for meaninglessness from their scientific and philosophical perspectives respectively, there is something unacceptable and unconvincing about what they say. For them, a piece of paper, for example, has more meaning than a human being, because at least it was manufactured for a purpose, unlike men and women.

It is a tragic thing to be deceived or deluded by our own imaginations. The problem with being deceived is that we never realize that we *are* deceived. The autobiography of Sir Alec Guinness, *Blessings in Disguise*, tells about an incident when he was playing Father Brown on location in Burgundy. Walking back to his lodgings one evening, still wearing his priest's costume, it grew dark:

> I hadn't gone far when I heard scampering footsteps and a piping voice calling, 'Mon Père!' My hand was seized by a boy of seven or eight, who clutched it tightly, swung it and kept up a non-stop prattle ... Although I was a total stranger he obviously took me for a priest and so to be trusted. Suddenly, with a 'Bonsoir Mon Père', and a hurried sideways sort of bow, he disappeared through a hole in the hedge. He had a happy, reassuring walk home, and I was left with an odd calm sense of elation ... [4]

There were two happy individuals, but their contentment was based on delusion. To keep God at a distance and to live as if he were dead or irrelevant may be the politically correct or socially acceptable thing to do. However, not only does it leave plenty of unanswered questions, it is self-delusion because God has revealed himself to us. He has done so in several ways, but principally through Jesus Christ and the Bible.[5]

A God who is

Basic to Christian belief is the conviction that God has revealed himself to humanity. We have all heard someone say, 'Well, my view of God is ...' The problem with such philosophizing is that there could be six billion individual ideas about God if we follow such notions. The Bible says that human beings were made in God's image, which was quite a compliment! It is an insult to God, though, if we try to make *him* in our image. When we ask the question, 'Why doesn't God stop everything that's wrong with the world?' we are making assumptions about the character of God. These assumptions may turn out to be true, but we have to be careful that the God we are questioning isn't one we have invented. It would be foolish to have a God of our own devising, who subsequently doesn't quite fit into all we would have imagined of him, causing us to dismiss the notion of a deity and regard ourselves as non-believers. I have often asked atheists the simple question, 'What sort of a God don't you believe in?' Having listened to their answer, I reply that I too would be an atheist if that's what God is like.

What God is like

The Bible teaches that God is a spirit who has all power, is all knowing, and is everywhere. He never changes, and he is totally just and infinitely loving. God is good. He is bigger than and beyond all things, and yet is interested and involved in the details of the things that concern us. As God, he does not *have* to explain himself to us. And yet he has made himself known to us.

As we read the words of Jesus and the Bible as a whole, we learn that there is only one God, who has a multiple personality. God is a triune God, who is Father, Son and Holy Spirit. God is personal, hence we call God 'him'. It is not that God has gender, but that he has personality. He feels and experiences emotions. Time and again in the Bible, we read that God is altogether wise, knowing and powerful. Paul, one of the main contributors to the New Testament part of the Bible, wrote:

Oh, the depth of the riches of the wisdom
    and knowledge of God!
  How unsearchable his judgments,
  and his paths beyond tracing out!
  'Who has known the mind of the Lord?
  Or who has been his counsellor?'[6]

The Bible makes it clear that God is altogether loving, patient and compassionate. He is absolutely pure and just. The Bible repeatedly teaches this; for example: 'Righteousness and justice are the foundation of your throne; love and faithfulness go before you.'[7]

Great and marvellous are your deeds,
    Lord God Almighty.
  Just and true are your ways,
    King of the ages.[8]

Mystery and certainty

All that we know about God is because of what he has revealed to us, and yet we do not understand all things. We only partly know, and we cannot put all the cogs of God's working together. This twin truth of mystery and certainty is the key to answering the question 'Why?' In the book of Deuteronomy in the Bible, we read: 'The secret things belong to the LORD our God, but the things revealed belong to us and to our children for ever, that we may follow all the words of this law.'[9]

If we could comprehend everything there was to understand about God, either he would not be God, or we would not be mere humans. Our finite, frail and often fickle minds are never going to fathom the depths of an infinite and eternal God.

There are things we will never be able to understand or explain. There are concepts and incidents that are beyond us. Christians believe that God is wise in his reservations as well as his revelations. Despite all the unanswered questions and bewildering issues of life, we have the solid character of God, who is totally reliable. There will always be a sense in

Our finite, frail and often fickle minds are never going to fathom the depths of an infinite and eternal God.

which Christians will be agnostic. We do not know or understand things as God does, and yet we have a firm confidence that God knows what he is doing and always does what is best. 'The God of Israel, the Saviour, is sometimes a God who hides himself, but never a God who absents himself; sometimes in the dark, but never at a distance.'[10] There are countless promises in the Bible on which Christians can rest, which give assurance. If some see these as a crutch, perhaps there is some truth in that idea, but then crutches can be very helpful to those who are injured!

Christian confidence and certainty, even in times of great suffering, is based not on an explanation from God as to why, but on the assurance of God's purpose and presence.

When Verna Wright, the eminent Professor of Rheumatology at Leeds University, was struggling with cancer, he experienced great comfort from the knowledge that God was in control, even though he himself might not have chosen the path allotted to him. Wanting to comfort his daughter, who also had cancer, he quoted the words of a hymn:

> I am not skilled to understand
> What God has willed, what God has planned;
> I only know at his right hand
>   Stands one who is my Saviour.[11]

Helen Roseveare, a missionary doctor, faced this tension between mystery and certainty, between the secret things and the revealed things. She studied medicine at Cambridge University, where she became a Christian through friends in the Christian Union. Eventually she went to the Belgian Congo (Zaire) to work as a missionary doctor. She personally supervised the building of a hospital compound and did remarkable work, not only in caring for patients, but in training medical auxiliaries and nurses. During the Congo uprising in 1964, she was captured by Simba rebels. Brutalized, raped and imprisoned, she was taken out of prison to be shot. She was miraculously granted a reprieve, however, and eventually escaped the Congo and returned to her home in the UK. When the uprising came to an end, despite all her ordeals, she went back to continue her work in the Congo. Naturally, there were huge physical and emotional scars, but reflecting on what had happened, she said, 'I came to the conclusion that I could thank the Lord for trusting me with suffering, even if he never tells me why I had to go through it.'[12]

As Christians, we dare to call God 'Father'. He is a personal God. Although we do not understand all things, we enjoy a relationship with God which is intimate and real. It is like a husband-wife relationship, or that of a parent and child. And as a child has trust in his or her father (although sometimes, in human relationships, this is a misplaced trust), likewise we, as believers, are confident that God knows best. The Bible gives us what is in effect a family secret: 'And we know that in all things God works for the good of those who love him, who have been called according to his purpose.'[13] Human beings are not God; we do not know everything, but we can trust in and have a relationship with God, who does know and is in control. We are not able to give an array of explanations to each individual's suffering, but God has revealed to us principles which offer insights, which may in turn help us to explain. As the prolific North American author Warren Wiersbe puts it, 'People live by promises and not by explanations.'[14] That belief is the basis for the famous quotation, 'All I have seen teaches me to trust the Creator for all I have not seen.'[15] Trusting that God knows best, even if we cannot fathom the intricacies of what is happening, leads us to a position where we can trust and feel at peace knowing that God is in control of all things.

Habakkuk lived as a prophet around 600 BC. He complained to God that his people were being badly abused by the Babylonians, and he could not understand God's apparent silence. God answered Habakkuk and turned his complaining into prayer and confidence in God, even if life was still 'unbearable'. Habakkuk's prophecy in the Bible ends with an upbeat song affirming his joy in God:

Though the fig-tree does not bud
  and there are no grapes on the vines,

though the olive crop fails
   and the fields produce no food,
though there are no sheep in the pen
   and no cattle in the stalls,
yet I will rejoice in the LORD,
   I will be joyful in God my Saviour.[16]

Part Two

Finding God in a
messed-up world

3. THE WORLD AS IT WAS

A world away from ours

The first book of the Bible, the book of Genesis, is the book of beginnings: the beginning of the universe, of planet Earth, of life, of the human race, of language, of family life, of civilization, of nations, of government. It also has the beginning of sin, suffering and death, and the beginning of the promise of forgiveness and reconciliation to God.

The opening, dramatic pages of the Bible portray a world very different from our own. In Genesis 1 we read how, day after day, God created, at the climax of each day pronouncing all that he had brought into being as 'good'. On the sixth day, when he made man and woman, God went further and pronounced creation as 'very good'. So humans, with our desires, drives, emotions and personalities, were seen as perfect from God's perspective. The paradise which God had created on earth had no sin, suffering, sickness, sadness or death. There was no struggle for existence, no cruelty, no pollution, no physical calamities such as floods, earthquakes, hurricanes or tsunamis; there was no imbalance – in either order or justice. Rather, the first humans lived their lives as companions and lovers, with nothing to hide from each other or God. They enjoyed God's presence with them, and he delighted in them. Harmony existed between heaven and earth. There was freedom, purity, security, love, trust and peace; concepts such as guilt, fear, evil, lust, selfishness, revenge and bitterness were alien to this world. If all this seems like a fairy tale, surely it is because we have become so distant from what God originally intended.

John Milton tried to describe how the world was and what Adam felt at the beginning of time. Here are the words Milton put in Adam's mouth as he spoke to the archangel Raphael:

> Hill, dale, and shady woods, and sunny plains,
> And liquid lapse of murmuring streams; by these,
> Creatures that live, and moved, and walked, or flew;
> Birds on the branches warbling; all things smiled.[1]

The Bible never seeks to prove the existence of God; it assumes it. The book of Genesis, and therefore the Bible, opens with the words, 'In the beginning God created the heavens and the earth.'[2] These are the words which were read to a listening world by the crew of the *Apollo 8* at Christmas 1968 after they had become the first humans to circumnavigate the moon. These simple words refute atheism, pantheism, polytheism, humanism and material-ism. Deism, the belief that God has made the world and left it to its own devices, is also discredited in the unfolding drama of the book of Genesis. Rather, the Bible teaches that God is intimately involved with all the details of our world, and with each individual within it.

Of course, it can be argued that as God knows everything he would have known what would happen, and he could have taken preventative measures. Why would God create an order that would become flawed and be the cause of so much human misery? Certainly God is not confined to or limited by time or space, so that the past, present and future are all known to him. In fact, the Bible speaks of Jesus and his crucifixion as ' . . . the Lamb that was slain from the creation of the world'.[3] Clearly, when the first human beings dared to defy God, shaking their fists in his face and rebelling against his explicit command, God was not taken by surprise. There was no emergency cabinet meeting in heaven in a desperate bid to find a solution to the problem. In what we can only call the wisdom of God, he knew what was to happen but did not remove our ability to disobey him. Without tying up all the ends, 1,700 years ago Augustine expressed what Christians believe today, that 'God judged it better to bring good out of evil than to suffer no evil to exist.'[4] There is a sense in which I am content to leave it there, as any attempt to explain the workings of God's infinite mind would be speculative. I dare not go beyond what God has revealed to us about himself. To do so would be to start to create my own god.

A wonderful world?

Despite all the wickedness and suffering in the world, there is still great beauty, kindness, loveliness, awe and wonder. They are all remnants of those things which characterized the world God made. Our emotions are stirred when we hear one of the greatest jazz musicians of all time, Louis Armstrong, sing of the colours in the rainbow, of friendship, or the wonder of human life, in 'What a wonderful world'. While we recognize that the world is marred, like

Louis Armstrong we see that it is also majestic. One of the distinguishing features of modern life is that we are bombarded with countless images of the horrors taking place around the world. Even Armstrong's song of celebration was set against the indescribable horrors of the Vietnam War portrayed in the 1987 film *Good Morning, Vietnam!* Images of atrocities are so commonplace on our TV screens and in our newspapers that our perception of reality can be eroded by the daily barrage of so constant a flow of such images. We can lose sensitivity to suffering through over-exposure to it and 'compassion fatigue' sets in. The danger then is that we can become duplicitous, apparently having the ability to show great sympathy one minute, but the next minute going on with our lives as if we have no cares in the world.

Leslie Davis, a North American journalist and Foreign Service Officer who worked in Turkey and Armenia at the beginning of the twentieth century, recognized this ability to follow Lord Nelson's example and raise a telescope to a blind eye. At first Davis wrote about 'how peacefully the Armenians and Turks were getting along'.[5] But not long after he would write about the genocide of the Armenian people, 'Who could have then foreseen, amid these peaceful surroundings, that the following year there was to be in this region what is probably the most terrible tragedy that has befallen any people in the history of the world?'[6] He described one of the perpetrators of the genocide, Sabit Bey, as having something sociopathic about his behaviour:

> I have seen tears roll down the cheeks of [him] at the imaginary
> sufferings of a young man who was playing the part of a
> wounded soldier in an amateur theatrical performance given for
> the benefit of the Turkish Red Crescent Society. Yet, a hundred

thousand people were made homeless and most of them
perished from violence as a result of his orders.[7]

Sometimes an act of kindness or sensitivity issues from even
the most evil of men. One thinks, if only their true character, the character that God created, had not been hijacked
by the cruel understudy of sin, how different they would be.
It is all too easy to express horror at the suffering and
injustice in the world, and yet contribute to the wrongs of
our world by selfish living. There is something great about
each human being, but also something absolutely awful.

4. THE WORLD TAKES A TURN

No longer perfect

The perfect world created by God was to be wrecked and ruined in an instant when the first man and woman deliberately disobeyed God, insisting that they should discover evil. The Bible graphically describes this moment, which was to change the face of history and take from us what would have been a very different world order.[1]

This deliberate act of defiance led to the first man and woman being expelled from the paradise of the Garden of Eden, to live in a world wrecked by the catastrophic consequences of sin. Their world would be characterized by a separation from God, as well as by suffering and death.

Although we do not know the ultimate origin of evil, we are told that it was never God's desire that human beings should discover or imbibe it. Outside Genesis 3 there is no explanation that makes sense of the mess and muddle which is endemic in our world. The Bible makes it clear that the world in which we now live is not as God desired or designed it to be. If incidents of suffering and wrongdoing leave *us* feeling hurt, they affect the loving and compassionate God in a far greater way. Time and again, as God reveals himself to us in the Bible, he demonstrates that he really does care, and that his heart leans towards us.

The Bible makes it clear that the world in which we now live is not as God desired or designed it to be.

Today, in the material realm, everything has a tendency to wear out and decay. In the living world animals as well as humans are engaged in a constant struggle against disease and predators, and they also are affected by ageing and death. Culturally, civilizations rise for a time and then crumble and die. In the spiritual and moral realm, we find it easier to do wrong than to do right. At several levels, our world is characterized by alienation and hence is full of hatred, crime, war, pollution, selfishness and dishonesty. Clearly, something has gone wrong with what was initially perfect.

An internal problem

The film *The Pianist*, directed and produced by Roman Polanski and starring Adrien Brody, features a Polish Jew who is an outstanding pianist, on the run from the Nazis. He owes his survival ultimately to a Nazi officer who shows compassion to him. In the original book, which led to the film, we are given extracts from the officer's diary. He is making the point that the origin of the world's atrocities lies in the individual human heart and our defiance against God:

1 September 1942

Why did this war have to happen at all? Because humanity had to be shown where its godlessness was taking it ...

There are no commandments now against stealing, killing or lying, not if they go against people's personal interest. This denial of God's commandments leads to all the other immoral manifestations of greed – unjust self-enrichment, hatred, deceit, sexual licence resulting in infertility and the downfall of the German people. God allows all this to happen, lets these forces have power and allows so many innocent people to perish to show mankind that without him we are only animals in conflict, who believe we have to destroy each other. We will not listen to the divine commandment: 'Love one another'. Very well, then, says God, try the Devil's commandment, the opposite: 'Hate one another'. We know the story of the Deluge from Holy Scripture. Why did the first race of men come to such a tragic end? Because they had abandoned God and must die, guilty and innocent alike. They had only themselves to blame for their punishment. And it is the same today.[2]

Innately evil

There are times when we are driven to the conclusion that the wickedness of certain actions is beyond rational human behaviour. For example, Dr Richard Badcock, a psychiatrist at Rampton Special Hospital near Retford, spent more than a hundred hours with Dr Harold Shipman, Britain's worst serial murderer. Shipman had worked as a family doctor in communities where he was trusted. Yet this seemingly inoffensive man was repeatedly murdering his patients. Badcock argued that Shipman was a 'classic necrophiliac', but added, 'Equally you make a case for it being a spiritual disorder. It is a disorder that transcends the conventional

disciplines of medicine, psychology and religion. It is something that presumably many could get into but don't. I think
evil comes into it.'[3]

However, in some circles to 'behave badly' has become an
acceptable, admirable and commendable thing. We recognize and repeat that we are all tarred with the same brush
and that 'nobody is perfect', but such attitudes are rarely a
humble admission that we are not the people we were
created to be. By nature, 'all have sinned and fall short of the
glory of God'.[4] There are Ten Commandments which not
only show us what is right, but also show us up for being
wrong at the very heart of our being. Jesus summarized the
Ten Commandments by saying that we should love the Lord
our God with all our heart, mind and soul, and that we
should love our neighbours as ourselves.[5] Not one of us can
claim to have lived in this way.

The blame game

When we are proved to be failing in some way, it is tempting
to argue that the root cause is somebody else's fault. It is an
old ploy. As some wag has said, 'Adam blamed Eve; Eve
blamed the serpent, and the serpent hadn't a leg to stand on.'
In more recent times, the classic demonstration of this was
at the Nuremberg Trials in 1945–9 where the Nazi war
criminals were indicted for their crimes against humanity.
Josef Seuss, an administrative assistant, whimpered, 'A soldier
can only carry out his orders.' Walter Langlesit, a battalion
commander, declared, 'I was just a little man. Those things
were done on orders from the big shots.' Colonel Hoess,
commandant of the notorious Auschwitz concentration
camp, who personally supervised the extermination of two
and a half million Jews, explained, 'In Germany it was
understood that if something went wrong, the man who

gave the orders was responsible. So I didn't think I would ever have to answer for it myself.' Hermann Goering, founder of the Gestapo and Luftwaffe, and formerly the second-ranking man in Germany, blustered, 'We had to obey orders.'

In August 2002 Holly Wells and Jessica Chapman, two ten-year-old girls from Soham, Cambridgeshire, were murdered. The crime seemed all the more horrific because the killer was actually a trusted friend known to the girls through school and living within walking distance of their home. Newspaper columnists wrote articles expressing horror at what had happened, but assuring their readers that we are not really bad, although once in a while there may be an outburst of wickedness. That is not how the Bible views us. Jesus, speaking about prayer, said, 'If you, then, though you are evil . . . '[6] As a result of what theologians call 'the fall', when the first human beings rebelled against the authority and will of God, we have inherited a nature which is inherently bad. That does not mean that we can do nothing commendable. There is still a joy in being involved in good works, but even they can be spoiled by wrong motives and pride. However, it does mean that we are each capable of disobeying God in ways that may hit the headlines or may simply harden our hearts. God has consistently hated sin; he never grows accustomed to it in the way that we do. By nature, he is absolutely truthful, clean and holy. He is impeccable in his purity, justice and goodness. He is without hypocrisy, duplicity and sham. By nature he cannot overlook our wrongdoing. How different from us.

North American television interviewer Mike Wallace introduced a programme about the Nazi Adolf Eichmann, a principal architect of the Holocaust. At the outset he posed a central question: 'How is it possible . . . for a man to act as

Eichmann acted? Was he a monster? A madman? Or was he perhaps something more terrifying: was he normal?'

The most startling answer to Wallace's shocking question came in an interview with Yehiel Dinur, a concentration camp survivor who testified against Eichmann in court. A film clip from Eichmann's 1961 trial showed Dinur walking into the courtroom and stopping short, after seeing Eichmann for the first time since the Nazi had sent him to Auschwitz eighteen years earlier. Dinur began to sob uncontrollably, then fainted, collapsing in a heap on the floor as the presiding judicial official pounded his gavel for order in the crowded courtroom.

Was Dinur overcome by hatred? Fear? Horrid memories?

No; it was none of these. Rather, as Dinur explained to Wallace, all at once he realized that Eichmann was not the godlike officer who had sent so many to their deaths. This Eichmann was an ordinary man. 'I was afraid about myself...' said Dinur. 'I saw that I am capable to do this. I am ... exactly like he.'[7]

'Eichmann is in all of us' is a sobering and horrifying thought. To confront evil, as Dinur did, can be a devastating experience. Nevertheless, as one reads the Bible, it is clear that God adamantly wants us to face the reality of who we are and what we are like. It is not God's intention to leave us cowering and guilt-ridden, but rather to forgive, transform and free us, making us the people we were created to be.

Warren Wiersbe notes:

There is something worse than suffering, and that is sin. Don't pity Jesus on the cross. Instead, pity Caiaphas, the scheming religious liar; or Pilate, the spineless Roman politician; or Judas, the money-grabbing thief who wasted the opportunity of a lifetime. We shed tears, and rightly so, for a loved one killed in

an accident; but too often we don't weep for the drunken driver
who caused the accident. We permit our suffering to blind us
to the real cause of suffering in this world – human rebellion
against God.[8]

However, that does not necessarily mean that the reason
one individual suffers more than another is that he or she
has done something particularly bad and therefore has
'displeased the gods'. Superstition or muddled religious
thinking can sometimes lead people who have been diagnosed with a serious illness, or who are going through
particularly difficult times, to believe they are being
punished. Jesus firmly dispelled such a notion. In John 9
we read:

> As [Jesus] went along, he saw a man blind from birth. His
> disciples asked him, 'Rabbi, who sinned, this man or his parents,
> that he was born blind?'
> 'Neither this man nor his parents sinned,' said Jesus, 'but this
> happened so that the work of God might be displayed in his
> life.'[9]

Jesus was not teaching that the man born blind and his
parents were sinless, for elsewhere he makes it very clear
that we are all sinful.[10] The point is that the sinful nature and
actions of the man and his parents did not directly lead to the
man's blindness. We are all caught up in the bundle of life,
and that means we may well find ourselves suffering or
struggling in one way or another. It is the world in which we
are living, rather than the things of which we are guilty, that
is the cause.

Our world has become a place where evil, injustice and
suffering prevail. Blaming individuals or powers does not

alleviate the hurt that is felt, nor does it provide answers as to the cause and cure of what is wrong. Nonetheless, to find the source of suffering may help to provide the remedy, relieve the pain and create hope for the future.

5. THE WORLD IS RESCUED

It is natural to wonder why God doesn't stop trouble in the world. If we are moved by the suffering of others, surely God must be too. Essentially, to begin to find an answer, we need to look at Jesus Christ's death and subsequent resurrection. Christians believe this is central to all understanding of what God is doing in the world, and his intervention – or otherwise – in the world's problems.

Christians believe that Jesus is Lord of all. He came from God the Father to planet Earth, living a pure life without sin or shame. Yet the people he loved so much plotted to execute him. *Why did God allow such callous cruelty? Why did God the Father desert his own Son at such a terrible time? Why did he not do something to intervene?*

God on earth
The Bible teaches that there is only one God. He is eternal, all-powerful, all-knowing, never changing, totally just and

loving, and he is everywhere. There is multiple personality in the Godhead, so that the one God is in three persons: Father, Son and Holy Spirit. While the three persons of the Trinity are one, they are also distinct. God the Son took on himself a human body and came into the world that he had created. He was coming to rescue us from the plight we had got ourselves into – the plight of separation from him.

Amongst the many names of Jesus is 'Immanuel', which means 'God with us'. The God of the universe was big enough to become small, strong enough to become weak. God may be distant in some respects, but he is also immanent, close to us, identifying himself and involving himself with the affairs of planet Earth. In fact, he is *in* the world. The opening of the Gospel of John, one of the Bible's biographies of Jesus, reads: 'In the beginning was the Word, and the Word was with God, and the Word was God . . . The Word became flesh and made his dwelling among us.'[1] It was God's plan that in the fullness of time he would step into the arena of human history to reach out to and rescue men and women.[2] The Creator became like us, his creation, as he clothed himself in a human body. God did not turn away from the suffering and sin of the world, nor did he wash his hands of it. Instead, he came to this earth, destined to suffer and die. Jesus, the Son of God, came alongside suffering humanity. As his mother was a virgin, and not married at the time she gave birth, he was probably branded as 'illegitimate'. The story of the birth of Christ is well known, but the reality was not as cosy as nativity plays make out. With no place to stay, Mary had to rest her newborn baby in an animal feeding trough. When Jesus was a child, his parents, Mary and Joseph, had to flee with him as refugees to Egypt, as King Herod ordered the killing of all baby boys in Bethlehem.

Jesus Christ knew what it was to be rejected, misunderstood, reviled, scorned and hated. After all the love and concern for individuals which Jesus showed, nevertheless he was called a Samaritan (a race despised at that time), a glutton, a wine-bibber, a friend of sinners, and he was even accused of being demon-possessed. He was mocked, spat upon, pierced by nails and blasphemed.

Among his twelve disciples, he deliberately chose one who was a traitor, and who eventually sold Jesus for the price of a slave, thirty pieces of silver. Political and religious leaders, who should have known better, dogged Jesus' footsteps, trying to trap and undermine him. Ultimately it was they who had Jesus crucified. It was for this that he was born. As novelist Dorothy Sayers put it, '[God] had the honesty and the courage to take his own medicine.'[3]

The bitterness and aggression that Jesus endured was despite the fact that he went around doing good. He spread an atmosphere of love and peace as he taught the world's highest moral standards. All that he taught was simply part of the standard set by the way he lived. He cured the sick, raised the dead, fed the hungry crowds and transformed for the good those who trusted him. He went alongside the underdogs of society, cared for those who were rejected and despised, lifted up the downtrodden and forgave sins.

Physical and emotional suffering

Eventually, though, Jesus was betrayed and arrested. He endured a mockery of a trial, where even his judge, Pontius Pilate, asked, 'Why? What crime has he committed?'[4] Pilate's wife sent a message to her husband saying, 'Don't have anything to do with that innocent man...'[5] The crowds howled for his death, really to try to hurt the hated Pilate rather than Jesus: 'Crucify him!'[6] and 'Let his blood be on us and on our children!'[7] Though symbolically washing his hands of the death of Jesus, Pilate gave the order and 'handed him over to be crucified'.[8]

They stripped Jesus and mocked him. His bare back was beaten so that it appeared like a ploughed-up field. The Roman soldiers twisted a crown of thorns and put it on his head. They put a reed in his hand, knelt in front of him and gave mock praise to him. They spat in his face, and struck him with the reed.

They then dressed him in ordinary clothes and made him carry his cross. He collapsed under the weight of it. No-one whom Jesus had helped or healed came to his assistance. Eventually, Simon of Cyrene was compelled to carry the cross for Jesus. When they arrived at the place called 'Golgotha', meaning 'The Place of the Skull', the soldiers crucified Jesus along with two criminals. On the cross, Jesus refused the wine offered to him, for as journalist Malcolm Muggeridge put it, 'Jesus refuses to swallow the drugged drink normally provided as an act of compassion to those about to be crucified; he has to be aware of his suffering. His supreme sacrifice, to be valid, must be conscious.'

Dramatic events occurred at the time of the crucifixion, but what was happening to Jesus himself was horrific. Jesus suffered physically in the same way as the other tens of thousands of people crucified by the Romans. A description of crucifixion and the slow and intensely painful death of those subjected to this form of execution should be read by those in doubt of whether Jesus really did suffer.

As well as suffering physically, Jesus suffered emotionally. His disciples, who had given up everything to follow him, now deserted him and fled. One betrayed him, another repeatedly denied him, and the others cowered in fear of what might happen to them. Cursing criminals were crucified on either side of him, and the howling mob of political and religious leaders and ordinary citizens hurled verbal abuse at him. The worst aspect of Christ's death on the cross, however, is that he also suffered spiritually.

Spiritual suffering

In all his teaching, Jesus repeatedly spoke of his death by crucifixion.[9] These were not the words of a gloomy pessimist. Jesus had come to die, and the ultimate purpose of his death was to take on himself the sin of the world. We read that Christ 'gave himself for our sins to rescue us from the present evil age, according to the will of our God and Father'.[10] The greatest work that Jesus would do was to die.

God, who is absolutely just, satisfied his justice against all the wrongdoing of the world as Jesus died on the cross. Jesus took on himself the sin of the world and God's rightful anger against it. Jesus died as the substitute sacrifice as he paid the penalty for our wrong, so that we might be forgiven and be declared free and forgiven by God. At the cross, God's love for us and his justice against sin met together.

At the cross, God's love for us and his justice against sin met together.

God, who hates all wrongdoing, took the sin of the world and laid it on Jesus. He paid for it so that we might be forgiven and so that the barrier of sin, which separates us from God, might be removed. It was the world's greatest act of love, 'For the grace of God that brings salvation has appeared to all men ... our great God and Saviour, Jesus Christ ... gave himself for us to redeem us from all wickedness and to purify for himself a people that are his very own, eager to do what is good.'[11] Jesus was made guilty so that we who are actually guilty might be forgiven. He carried the can for our sin, so that all our guilt might be removed. Our unrighteousness was laid on Jesus the sinless one, so that we could be declared sinless in the sight of God.

When the late Pope John Paul II saw a preview version of Mel Gibson's film *The Passion of the Christ*, it was reported that he said, 'It is as it was.'[12] However, although it may successfully have portrayed Christ's physical sufferings, no-one can ever depict Jesus' death as it was. The significance of the cross of Jesus lies not only in his physical or emotional sufferings, but in his act of carrying the weight of the world's sin on himself. God transformed what appeared to be a sad and tragic end to a good life into what was to be the greatest benefit for the world. Jesus is the Saviour who himself has suffered and gone through death. God devised a means whereby we who should be banished can be brought near to him through the achievement of the sacrifice of his Son.

As Christ was suffering, '[He] cried out in a loud voice, *"Eloi, Eloi, lama sabachthani?"* – which means, "My God, my God, why have you forsaken me?"'[13] God turned away from his Son because Jesus was made 'to be sin for us'.[14] He was forsaken by God, so that we might be forgiven and never forsaken by God. He took our separation from God on himself, so that we could know and experience God's presence through all life's journey. As Jesus entered the hours of suffering on the cross, he prayed: 'Father, forgive them, for they do not know what they are doing.'[15] When Jesus had paid for our sin and was about to give up his life, he prayed in a loud voice: 'Father, into your hands I commit my spirit.'[16] The Bible records that after crying out these words, he breathed his last breath. As he was bearing the sin of the world, he could only speak to God as God, and not as his Father. Mysteriously and wonderfully, such was the

horrendous happening of Jesus dying for us that a separation
of the Father and Son occurred. Out of love for us, and a
desire that we be freed from the mess we are in, Jesus took
on himself all that should be ours – including the gulf
between us and God. He became our substitute.

Forgiveness offered to all

Whatever our sins, there is forgiveness for all who genuinely
and sincerely turn from those sins to God, who is infinitely
merciful. Guilt creates its own suffering. Albert Speer was a
confidant of Hitler whose technological genius was credited
with keeping Nazi factories humming throughout World
War 2. He was the only one of the twenty-four criminals
tried at Nuremberg to admit his guilt. Speer spent twenty
years in Spandau prison. He later said, 'I served a sentence
of twenty years, and I could say, "I'm a free man, my
conscience has been cleared by serving the whole time as
punishment." But I can't do that. I still carry the burden of
what happened to millions of people during Hitler's lifetime,
and I can't get rid of it.'[17] His writings are filled with
contrition and warnings to others to avoid his moral sin. He
desperately wanted expiation. Because of what Jesus accomplished on the cross, there is the offer of forgiveness for those
who will repent and believe. As the Bible expresses it, 'the
blood of Jesus, [God's] Son, purifies us from all sin ... If we
confess our sins, he is faithful and just and will forgive us our
sins and purify us from all unrighteousness.'[18]

Power over death

God's ability to transform the worst situation is demonstrated in Jesus' death and resurrection. After his death, he
was taken by friends and buried in a previously unused
tomb. There his body, wrapped in cloths, lay cold, still, dead.

The tomb was sealed, and guarded by Roman soldiers. For three days and nights he lay in the cave. Then, on the first 'Easter morning', the light of the rising sun revealed that the stone had been rolled away and the body of Jesus had gone, even though strips of linen were lying there, as well as the separate burial cloth that had been around Jesus' head.[19] Jesus had risen from the dead. This was no 'conjuring trick with bones'.[20] There is a huge amount of evidence from Christian, Jewish and Roman writers of the day testifying to the supernatural happenings around the death and resurrection of Jesus.[21] It is an aspect of the life of Jesus Christ that marks him out as being utterly unique. It demonstrates God's power to bring life out of death and victory out of apparent defeat.

In an interview broadcast through the world's media on 23 December 2003, Samantha Roberts, the widow of the first British soldier killed in the Iraq war, told how she had met President George W. Bush when he had made a state visit to the UK a month earlier. She recalled standing before 'the most powerful man on the earth' and then added, 'But he couldn't bring back my husband.' Only Jesus, who is 'the way and the truth and the life',[22] could not allow himself to be taken hostage, even by death. Those who put their faith and trust in Christ find that by his Holy Spirit he gives life – life that takes a person through death and into eternity with him.

6. THE WORLD AS IT WILL BE

When Jesus began his three years of preaching, healing and teaching, he chose twelve men to train. They were to be with him in all his work. The youngest of these was John, who was to outlive the others. He is the author of the Gospel of John, plus some letters found in the New Testament and the final book of the whole Bible, the book of Revelation. John was imprisoned for his faith in Christ on the island of Patmos in the Mediterranean Sea. On this desolate island, surrounded by the surging sea, it is as if God pulled back a curtain to give John a glimpse of eternity. The book of Revelation, which describes this, has to be the greatest futurama of all time. Towards the end of the vision which John describes, he saw the new heaven and the new earth:

> Then I saw a new heaven and a new earth, for the first heaven and the first earth had passed away, and there was no longer any sea. I saw the Holy City, the new Jerusalem, coming down out

of heaven from God, prepared as a bride beautifully dressed for her husband. And I heard a loud voice from the throne saying, 'Now the dwelling of God is with men, and he will live with them. They will be his people, and God himself will be with them and be their God. He will wipe every tear from their eyes. There will be no more death or mourning or crying or pain, for the old order of things has passed away.'

He who was seated on the throne said, 'I am making everything new!' Then he said, 'Write this down, for these words are trustworthy and true.'

He said to me: 'It is done. I am the Alpha and the Omega, the Beginning and the End. To him who is thirsty I will give to drink without cost from the spring of the water of life. He who overcomes will inherit all this, and I will be his God and he will be my son. But the cowardly, the unbelieving, the vile, the murderers, the sexually immoral, those who practise magic arts, the idolaters and all liars – their place will be in the fiery lake of burning sulphur. This is the second death.'[1]

This graphic description is of something which seems alien to us. Nobody likes tears, and in heaven God will wipe away all tears. We don't particularly like darkness, and in heaven there will be no more night. We go to great lengths to avoid pain, and in heaven there will be no more pain. We hate death, and in heaven nobody dies. We dislike any kind of sorrow, and the inhabitants of heaven do not weep. No-one likes separation, and in heaven there will be no more sea, the ultimate symbol of separation. It is a place of unclouded day, where God's reign and goodness are supreme.

This means that death can be a moment of release for some. Only God holds the keys of death, so to take the life of an individual to relieve his or her suffering is to play God – and that cannot be right. Nevertheless, there are times when one looks on a situation where there has been a death and finds comfort in the thought that the deceased has gone to be with God and is relieved of suffering.

Hanse Cronje had for six years been the greatly loved and respected South African cricket captain. He was a genuine Christian believer. Foolishly, he became involved in match fixing and was banned from playing representative cricket for life. On 1 June 2002 he was killed in a plane crash. Surprisingly, Cronje's mother later suggested that perhaps it had been a blessing that her son had died. She said that he had suffered so much, had lost all his confidence and would have had to bear the consequences of the match-fixing scandal for the rest of his life. Cricket coach Ali Bacher said, 'That summed up the whole tragedy for me; a mother suggesting that only in death could her son be freed from his burden.'[2] Her confidence that things would be better for her son after death was clearly not based on the thought that he was good enough for heaven, but on the fact that he was trusting Christ to forgive all that would condemn him.

Eternal trouble

Most of us give little time to considering even the possibility of an afterlife. Yet it is something we should not ignore. The passage in the book of Revelation also teaches that there is a place of eternal trouble. The Bible warns of hell, a punishment after life on earth. God is absolutely just and righteous. Rejection of him and his ways has a penalty. Jesus, who loved so much, warned that God, who is by nature just, must punish sin. There is ultimate justice. So we read that those who are unbelieving in mind and actions, those who have rejected God's remedy for forgiveness and reconciliation with himself, will pay their own penalty for their own sin. They have refused the gift of eternal life through Jesus Christ the Lord, and therefore receive the consequences of their sin.[3] It is hard to imagine a more serious theme.

Gwyn Williams was for some time a pastor of a church in Port Talbot in Wales. He was once given a tour of their famous steelworks. He was walking high up on a gantry when the guide revealed how a man had fallen from there into the 3,000 degrees of white heat of the furnace below. Gwyn Williams tried to imagine the horror of the man as he fell and thought that to be drawn into the holiness of God without the protection of Christ must be something similar.

Jesus himself, out of love, warned of the consequences of stubbornly refusing him; not for his own selfish or egotistical purposes, but because he longed for people to enjoy God and his creation in the way he intended it. His heart's desire was towards people, even though they may be extremely wayward. After exposing and berating the hypocrisy of the religious leaders of his day in Jerusalem, Jesus cried, 'O Jerusalem, Jerusalem, you who kill the prophets and stone those sent to you, how often I have longed to gather your children together, as a hen gathers her chicks under her wings, but you were not willing.'[4]

If God is just, and he has revealed himself as being just, then we would expect God to act fairly and finally towards those who reject him and choose to live contrary to the ways and laws that he has shown. There is something in human minds, also, which demands that there be more than simply the tame punishments of society's courts towards grossly wicked people. It does not seem right that Hitler could bring his existence to an end simply by pulling a trigger. He, along with millions of others, will be judged by God; their eternal destiny will depend on what they have done with God and the gift of salvation which he offered to them. Every nation, leader and individual will appear before God, who will be their judge.

Towards the end of the Bible there is a graphic vision of God's courtroom:

> Then I saw a great white throne and him who was seated on it. Earth and sky fled from his presence, and there was no place for them. And I saw the dead, great and small, standing before the throne, and books were opened. Another book was opened, which is the book of life. The dead were judged according to what they had done as recorded in the books. The sea gave up the dead that were in it, and death and Hades gave up the dead that were in them, and each person was judged according to what he had done. Then death and Hades were thrown into the lake of fire. The lake of fire is the second death. If anyone's name was not found written in the book of life, he was thrown into the lake of fire.[5]

The North American Jewish rabbi Harold S. Kushner caused a stir with his book entitled *When Bad Things Happen to Good People*. He had put his finger on how unfair suffering can be. However, bad things can happen to bad people too. Life is to be seen not merely from a current perspective, but from God's vantage point, which is an eternal view of events. Yet there is a brighter side to eternity that can transform the heart and mind of any who will turn from all that is wrong in their lives and trust Jesus Christ as their Lord, Saviour and friend. For the Christian there is no need to fear death. The 'sting' of death is our sin, but Christ has taken that sting himself, and therefore there is nothing of which to be afraid.

Future perspective

In AD 155, the city of Smyrna was the scene of religious amusement. Statius Quadratus, the Roman proconsul, was the guest of honour. As part of the entertainment, eleven Christians were brought in from Philadelphia to be thrown to the lions. The excitement of the people reached its peak. 'Polycarp! Polycarp!' they yelled. They searched for the greatly loved Christian leader. When he was found he was brought to the stadium. The proconsul tried in vain to persuade Polycarp to deny the lordship of Jesus Christ, but only received the reply: 'Eighty-six years I have served him, and he never did me wrong. How can I blaspheme my King who has saved me?' He was tied to a stake, flaming wood was placed on his aged body, and there he was martyred. His remains were buried on Mount Pagus.[6]

Having an eternal, future perspective on life means attempting to see the world as God sees it. The effect of this is startling. For example, in Psalm 73 the writer, Asaph, begins with an affirmation that God is good to his people, but then articulates the serious questions

Having an eternal, future perspective on life means attempting to see the world as God sees it.

that had caused doubts in his mind. Asaph could not be ostrich-like and bury his head in the sand; there were things that perplexed him. It seemed to him that wicked people prospered while those who tried to follow the laws of God did so in vain, because they suffered. He honestly and frankly tells God his concerns. It seems at first as though his doubts will lead to cynicism, but then there comes a change. The questioning continues until a moment in the psalm that is pivotal. Asaph begins to look at the situation from an eternal point of view. He ponders not only the life of people on earth, but their eternity, and the blessing that God gives to those who trust in him. He realizes that the snapshots of society with which he was being confronted are not the full story. In contrast to God, he is not everywhere, at all times. Not all Asaph's questions are answered, but enjoying the fact that God is close to him enables him to rest in renewed confidence that God knows what he is doing. Asaph revels in the fact that God is a precious friend to him and he is more significant than anything else. He says, with renewed confidence, 'Whom have I in heaven but you? And earth has nothing I desire besides you.'[7] He ends his psalm with the words, 'But as for me, it is good to be near God. I have made the Sovereign LORD my refuge; I will tell of all your deeds.'[8] And there he rests.

Part Three

Living with God in a
messed-up world

7. CHANGE

Leo Tolstoy was an orphaned son of a Russian nobleman. He left his university studies without a degree, fought in the Crimean War, wrote several acclaimed short novels, and experimented with progressive education for children – all before he married the eighteen-year-old Andreyevna Bers in 1862. The couple raised nineteen children. He is particularly remembered for his two great novels *War and Peace* and *Anna Karenina*. In an autobiographical note he wrote:

> Five years ago I came to believe in Christ's teaching, and my life suddenly changed; I ceased to desire what I had previously desired, and began to desire what I formerly did not want. What had previously seemed to me good seemed evil, and what seemed evil seemed good. It happened to me as it happens to a man who goes out on some business and on the way suddenly decides that the business is unnecessary and returns home. All

that was on his right is now on his left, and all that was on his
left is now on his right; his former wish to get as far as possible
from home has changed into a wish to be as near as possible to
it. The direction of my life and my desires became different, and
good and evil changed places . . .

I, like the thief [on the cross], knew that I was unhappy and
suffering. I, like the thief on the cross, was nailed by some force
to a life of suffering and evil. And as, after the meaningless
sufferings and evils of life, the thief awaited the terrible darkness
of death, so did I await the same thing . . .

But suddenly I heard the words of Christ and understood
them, and life and death ceased to seem evil, and instead of
despair I experienced happiness and the joy of life undisturbed
by death.[1]

Many Christians in vastly different cultures, ages and situations have experienced a similar distinct change of heart and
mind as they surrendered their life and future to Jesus Christ.
Their life, from that moment, with its highs and lows, would
never be the same.

Being a Christian essentially means being a follower of
Jesus Christ. This not only involves trusting in him as Lord
and Saviour, but following his example and attitude to this
broken world. In the Bible we read, 'if anyone is in Christ, he
is a new creation; the old has gone, the new has come!'[2]
Christians experience not only forgiveness from sin, but a
new perspective on life. They see beyond the immediate and
can look forward to a new world – a new creation
encompassing heaven and earth. In this new world people
will be reconciled to God and to one another through Jesus
Christ. A taste of this new world should be evident in the
way that Christians relate to each other and to the world
around them.

Cultivating relationship

There are those who say cynically that Christianity is merely a psychological prop. Christianity is much more than this. It is a vibrant relationship with God himself, which prepares and takes a person through each season of life. God may be called upon at any moment, but those who know him in the stable times of life are the ones who are ready for the storms of life.

Todd Beamer, who was on United Airlines Flight 93 bound for San Francisco on 11 September 2001, had such a relationship with God. When the plane was hijacked, he was the one who spoke those now immortal words, 'Let's roll!', as the passengers set about taking on the hijackers. Shortly afterwards, the plane crashed in a remote area of Pennsylvania. His widow later told how she found on their computer Todd's description of his relationship with God:

> I have had stops and starts in building my relationship with God
> . . . I screw up, I let him down, and I do not always spend time
> with God the way I should. This is because I am trying to force
> the relationship and steer it in the direction I want
> it to go. That doesn't work, and only leads to frustration.
>
> However, each time I come to God to ask for forgiveness, he
> is there for me. Each time I ask God for help, he is there for me.
> Each time I cry out in frustration and pain, he is there for me.
>
> While my relationship with God is far from perfect . . . God
> has been there for me time and again, and has expressed his love
> and grace for me. Although at times I have taken God for
> granted . . . my experience has been that God is patient and
> waiting for us to come to him. Once we come to him and give
> more of our lives to him, he will give more of himself to us.[3]

Not every Christian faces such dramatic circumstances, but we each face the reality of death. Having a relationship with

God, through Jesus Christ, means that death can be faced with confidence. For Christians death is not the end; it is the beginning of an eternity with the God they know and trust.

A friend of mine, Peter Frost, was a committed Christian. He worked in business and was married to Kathy, with whom he had a young son, Jonah. There was always something a little mischievous about this constantly cheerful man. When he was in his early thirties, however, he was diagnosed with leukaemia. The medical upheavals he faced as a consequence formed an unenviable period in his life, but during this painful time he developed a most intimate knowledge of God. A few months before he died, he wrote a short note to me:

11 March 2003

Dear Roger,

Just a quick note to say that I was admitted for a bone marrow transplant. I am at the Heath Hospital in Cardiff and expect to be here for a month or so (in isolation). It is a miracle that we have come this far – especially since my total relapse last November. At that stage this 'window of opportunity' was not open to us, but graciously [God] has brought us to this place.

We don't know what the short or medium term outcome will hold for us, but we do hope – not in an outcome, but in a Person. I was reading in Hebrews 6:16–20 – Jesus promises to us 'in his own name and he cannot lie'. 'We have this hope as an anchor for the soul, firm and secure . . .' I was reading an old Welsh hymn the other day and the last two lines of each verse read: 'too wise to make mistakes; too good to be unkind' . . .

Peter

Changing perspective

Some of the most wonderful words of comfort found in the Bible are right at the end, in the penultimate chapter of the book of Revelation. The ageing disciple John is describing the close of his vision, when he saw the new heavens and the new earth. He records the words of God himself, as heard in the vision:

> Now the dwelling of God is with men, and he will live with
> them. They will be his people, and God himself will be
> with them and be their God. He will wipe every tear from
> their eyes. There will be no more death or mourning or crying
> or pain, for the old order of things has passed away.[4]

Those who are trusting in Christ as their only way of reconciliation to God will indeed be reconciled to him. God will live with them, in a new world which is free from pain, suffering, disaster, disappointment, fear, brutality, grief, death, inequality, poverty and injustice. It is hard to imagine something so perfect and unspoilt, but it is a promise from the mouth of God himself, and it is offered to anyone who accepts God's desire to rescue us from the mess of this world.

There is such freedom and relief in knowing that ultimately, whatever life appears to deal to a person, something better is coming. Although God's judgment is real, heaven is guaranteed to everyone who has come to know God in their lives. Lord Hailsham, twice Lord Chancellor, and therefore the highest judge in Great Britain, expressed this well when he said, 'When I die and stand before God in judgment, I will plead guilty and cast myself upon the mercy of the court.' The assurance of heaven, freed from God's judgment, is the *incentive* that gives hope, the *comfort* that gives strength and the *confidence* that gives calm.

CASE STUDY I

Names: *Dave and Jan*

Situation: *Married couple with four young children, two of whom have a rare degenerative disease*

Dave and Jan met at university, where Dave was studying engineering and Jan medicine. During their first year of study, through different circumstances, they became Christians. They both realized that they had a problem of wrong within themselves, and their most pressing need was to respond to God's love for 'sinners', expressed through the death of Jesus Christ on the cross. Becoming Christians made a huge difference to them, as they experienced God's forgiveness in their lives. They began to read the Bible and see its relevance to their lives. Not long after graduation, they were married and set up home.

They had four children within five years. Hannah was first, followed closely by Amy, Josh and finally Daniel. At first things seemed as normal as they could be with young children in the home, but when Amy was about three, Dave and Jan began to realize that her development was different from that of her older sister Hannah. She appeared to be hyperactive, had continual ear problems and never slept through the night. She would often wake up, sometimes ten times a night, and then really struggle to get back to sleep. 'Although things didn't seem quite right,' they explain, 'we were not particularly concerned, as we had no idea of the underlying problem.'

Amy eventually started nursery school and then moved on into reception class at primary school. She was always affectionate and very popular with pupils and teachers alike. It was during this year, however, that her problems became more noticeable as she started to fall further behind her peers at school. She could barely put a few words together, would only scribble and did not concentrate on the tasks she was given to do.

During this year Dave and Jan were referred to a local paediatrician. They suspected that he realized what the problem was as soon as he saw Amy, but over the next few months he carried out various tests on all the family. Samples were sent off to Great Ormond Street Children's Hospital for analysis. During one of their appointments, the paediatrician hinted that he thought the problem was a rare genetic disorder. He was awaiting confirmation, he said.

During the weeks that followed, life continued relatively normally, but gradually Jan started to believe that there was something seriously wrong. And so began the roller-coaster emotions as the family faced the fact that Amy would not have a 'normal' life. As a Christian, Jan believed that God was in control, but the pain was still real.

At a later appointment with the paediatrician he confirmed what was suspected: Amy had Sanfilippo Syndrome, MPS (mucopolysaccharide) Type III(b), one of a family of rare genetic disorders. Not only did Amy, who was now nearly six, have Sanfilippo Syndrome, but Daniel, who was almost three, had the same disease. Jan looked in her medical textbooks to find out more about the condition, but there was very limited information as the condition was so rare. Over the next few days they learned more about the implications of Sanfilippo for the lives of Amy and Daniel. The paediatrician, trying to break the news gently, called at their house the following evening with a leaflet from the MPS Society, a national support group, telling more about what to expect in the future.

The life of a child with Sanfilippo can generally be divided into three phases. The first few years appear as fairly normal development. In the following years they become extremely hyperactive, but development levels off and they do not acquire the skills expected. The final stage is a degenerative phase during which they slow down, lose speech, mobility and all other skills. Average life expectancy is around fourteen years.

The days and weeks that followed the diagnosis were not easy. Coming to terms with the fact that two of their four children had a serious problem with a limited life expectancy was tough. Dave and Jan appreciated the support from the MPS Society as they helped them through some of the practical considerations and adjustments that had to be made, both then and in the following years. Family and friends were good to them, although it was often difficult for them as they too had to face up to the shock of what Dave and Jan had already started to go through.

'Through it all there was something else, which supported us and kept us going. We were acutely aware of the presence of God in a very real way,' says Dave. 'While at university we had both come to trust in Christ for forgiveness of sin. Since then he had made a real difference in our lives as we tried, with his help, to walk with him and live for him. Now, in the midst of difficult times, we had a great sense of his strengthening and upholding hand upon our lives. Although we couldn't understand why this should happen to us, we found that we were able to trust God fully. We are confident that God does not make mistakes and that although things can be difficult, he is with us in the difficulties.'

Over the years since they were first diagnosed with Sanfilippo, Amy and Daniel have continued to deteriorate. Amy (now nineteen) cannot talk or walk without help. Daniel (now sixteen) has very little speech and limited mobility. Both of them are totally dependent on others. They cannot make their needs known or feed themselves. They have no idea of the problems that they have. However, both of them are extremely affectionate and continue to be a great joy to Dave, Jan, Hannah and Josh, as well as to others who know them.

Reflecting on their situation, Jan says, 'We have continued to know [God's] help in recent years. It hasn't always been easy, but God has been good. We have had to learn to take one day at a time and to trust God day by day. As we look back we are overwhelmed by the goodness of God through it all, and as we anticipate difficult days ahead, our trust is in God who hasn't failed us in the past.'

8. COMFORT

Three months before he died, I received a letter from Professor David Short, the retired Professor of Medicine at Aberdeen University, who had been the Queen's Physician in Scotland. After some pleasantries, he wrote:

> A few days before setting out on our winter holiday in Spain, my wife and I got a health shock. We haven't time to tell all our friends the news but we would like you to hear it direct from us. A routine blood test showed that I had acute myeloid leukaemia. The consultant haematologist discussed treatment, and felt that current radical therapy is more trouble than it is worth. Whatever is done, the prognosis is measured in weeks or months. The holiday in [Spain] was perfect and at present I remain as well as ever.

He then quoted first the Bible and then the Victorian preacher and author C. H. Spurgeon, who saw death like crossing a river:

Isaiah 43, verses 1, 2 come to me with great comfort at this time.
'Fear not, for I have redeemed you . . . you are mine. When
you pass through the waters, I will be with you; and when you
pass through the rivers, they will not sweep over you.' And
Spurgeon's comment: 'There is no bridge and no ferry-boat.
We must go through the waters and feel the rush of the river.
The presence of God in the flood is better than a ferry-boat. The
sorrows of life may rise to an extraordinary height, but the Lord
is equal to every occasion. We are precious to God. He paid an
incalculable price for our salvation. We belong to him. Since he
paid so much for us, he is never going to part with us. Whatever
happens, he will be with us.'

Changing the metaphor, David Short then closed his letter
by saying:

We would both value your prayers: that I may be enabled to run
the last lap well and that Joan may have special help from [God].

Facing grief

Grief is the heaviness of heart caused by loss. It comes
uninvited and is not in a hurry to leave us. The Bible teaches
that it is only a matter of time before it is our turn to mourn.
Its effects are draining, debilitating and even destructive. The
loss is not necessarily of a person, but may be of a job, health
or reputation.

Grief is both natural and right, provided it doesn't become
self-pitying or vengeful. The need to grieve and express
profound sorrow is entrenched deep within the human
psyche. The pain caused by loss can be overwhelming,
numbing and relentless.

Everyone's grief is unique and individual. Some recover
more quickly, others need lots of time. King David, whose

story is told in the Bible, lost a baby son and an adult son. He recovered quickly after the baby's death, but the death of Absalom was very destructive to him. In fact, the Bible has stories of those grieving over the loss of a child, a sibling, a monarch or political leader, a spouse and a friend dying before there was a chance to say goodbye. Whatever the situation, we are never the same again after such losses. Like a person who has had a limb amputated, we can learn to live with the loss, but we are not going to be as we were before.

And yet people have found, like David Short and his wife Joan, that it is possible to have confidence in the crisis of death, both before and after bereavement. That certainty is given as a person faces death, and as another reflects on the loss that is causing so much hurt. The knowledge that God exists, that he is at the centre of everything, in control of all events and circumstances, and that he has defeated death through the death and resur-rection of Jesus, is wonderfully reassuring.

There is calm and rest in remembering that God is too wise to make mistakes and too good to be unkind.

There is calm and rest in remembering that God is too wise to make mistakes and too good to be unkind. That doesn't mean that there is no need to grieve or sorrow. God doesn't make those who trust him hard-nosed, insensitive autonomists. Instead, God promises to be with his children, to give them the resources to cope with their hurts, to heal the broken-hearted.

The importance of relationships is never seen so dramat-ically as when one is faced with loss and bereavement. There can be regrets over words said or unsaid, over wrong priorities, over actions and failures, over lack of intimacy or time with the person who has gone. In moments of such grief, it is best to be honest with God and tell him all our thoughts and regrets. The Bible encourages us to cast our cares on God knowing that he cares for us.[1] If the cause of our grief seems arbitrary, meaningless and unfair, we can give the questions and issues to God in prayer. In time he may explain what we are going through, but in the meantime we can at least trust him as we go through the sorrow.

Jesus drank deeply from the cup of suffering as he faced crucifixion. As a weightlifter concentrates intensely before actually attempting to lift the bars, so Jesus prayed before his execution in a garden called Gethsemane. The name Gethsemane means 'oil press'. It was a place where Jesus often went, and the name seemed to illustrate his life and death, as he was to be crushed. He was shortly to know what it was to experience every ounce of life being pressed out of him. We read that, while praying, his sweat was like drops of blood falling to the ground, such was the intensity of his suffering. Then, after Gethsemane, came Golgotha or 'The Place of the Skull' – the hill where Jesus was crucified. The darkness which Jesus went through on the cross means that he can sympathize with, encourage and strengthen all who feel forsaken in the mire of grief. He is able to draw alongside those who are discouraged, who feel there is little point to going on with life. That is exactly what he did with two of his followers after the events of his death and resurrection.

They were walking from Jerusalem to Emmaus, a journey of seven miles. Utterly downcast and despondent because of the events that had led to Jesus' crucifixion in the last few days, they were now confused because of the rumours that Jesus had risen from the dead. It was all too much for them. They had thought that Jesus was the one who was going to rescue Israel from the iron grip of the Roman Empire which was oppressively occupying their nation. Instead, he had been callously crucified.

Then a stranger began to walk with them. The Bible says that they were prevented from recognizing him. He appeared ignorant of all that had gone on, so the two travellers quickly took their opportunity to retell the story and express their bitter disappointment. Jesus walked and listened before turning first to rebuke them for their slowness to believe and then, from the Old Testament, to explain that what had happened was what had been prophesied. They later said their hearts were 'burning within' them[2] as Jesus opened the Scriptures to them, opened their minds so that they could understand those Scriptures, and then opened their eyes so that they could recognize him. Once these two followers of Jesus and his disciples began to understand that what had happened to Jesus was prophesied long before, they received great peace and happiness. Jesus said, 'This is what is written: The Christ will suffer and rise from the dead on the third day, and repentance and forgiveness of sins will be preached in his name to all nations...'[3]

Grief is such a nasty pain. It is hard to imagine any palliative that might cure the hurt, but without wanting to be at all glib, there is help even in such a time of trouble in the person of Jesus Christ. The apostle Paul, who penned so much of our New Testament, wrote to the fledgling church in Thessalonica reminding them that 'we do not want you to be ignorant about those who [die], or to grieve like the rest of men, who have no hope'.[4] He then explained that the death and rising again of Jesus, coupled with the certainty that one day Jesus will return as Lord and ruler of all, gives cause for great comfort, when one would naturally sorrow.

Finding comfort

The book of Psalms, in the middle of the Bible, is an ancient book of songs and praise to God. Reading through the 150 psalms, one finds a recurring dual theme: life is tough, but God is good. Over the centuries, thousands of people have found comfort through reading and meditating on the Psalms.

In Psalm 42 the author is going through dark times. He wisely speaks to his innermost being and reminds himself not to doubt in the darkness what God had shown him in brighter times.

> Why are you downcast, O my soul?
>   Why so disturbed within me?
> Put your hope in God,
>   for I will yet praise him,
>   my Saviour and my God.[5]

A couple of sentences later we read:

> By day the LORD directs his love,
>   at night his song is with me –
>   a prayer to the God of my life.[6]

The idea of 'songs in the night', or comfort in the darkest of times, has been the experience of many Christians. Paul and Silas, early followers of Jesus Christ, were imprisoned for their faith in Philippi. They had been beaten and put in a damp, cold prison. Yet we read that at midnight they sang praises to God.[7]

In Psalm 42 we also read the phrase 'the God of my life'. That phrase occurs only once in the whole Bible. The psalmist devised a new name for God, one which expressed his confidence that God knew what he was doing. He trusted

God, even though times were hard and the emotional structure that normally kept him in place had crumbled, leaving him totally despondent.

A favourite traditional Christian hymn is called 'It is well with my soul'. It was written by Horatio Spafford, a successful Chicago lawyer. In 1873 the Spaffords' family doctor recommended a holiday for Mrs Spafford, so the couple made plans to travel to Europe by ship. Just before leaving, Horatio Spafford had to change his plans and quickly arranged for his wife and four daughters to go ahead, promising to join them some days later. So his wife and the girls set sail without him.

On 22 November, in a tragic, freak accident, the ship was rammed and sank in less than half an hour. Mrs Spafford was rescued, but all four daughters were drowned. Later Mrs Spafford was able to cable her husband with the stark two-word message: 'Saved alone.'

Horatio Spafford bought passage on the first ship he could find that was sailing to England. At sea, as the ship crossed the Atlantic where his daughters' bodies lay, with tears in his eyes, he penned these words:

> When peace like a river attends my way
> When sorrows like sea billows roll;
> Whatever my lot, you have taught me to say:
> It is well, it is well with my soul.[8]

There is real comfort to be found when we trust that God is in control and we have put things right with him. It is possible to have absolute confidence in Jesus, who said, 'I am the resurrection and the life. He who believes in me will live, even though he dies; and whoever lives and believes in me will never die.'[9]

Developing empathy

In 1944 Corrie ten Boom was taken with her family to Ravensbrück concentration camp. They had been found hiding Jews in their home in Haarlem in Holland. Most of her family died very quickly, but she and her sister Betsie survived longer. Eventually, though, Betsie was to die after being brutalized and cruelly treated. Before she died, she said to Corrie, 'If ever you get out of this place, go and tell the world that no matter how deep the pit, God is deeper still.' For forty years that is exactly what Corrie did. Her autobiography, *The Hiding Place*, honestly recalls how God met with her and blessed her in the traumas of Ravensbrück.

This in no way means that Christians can gloss over such terrors and dismiss the injustice of them, simply because somebody had a spiritual experience. Nevertheless, in the midst of suffering people can find real and tangible comfort in the presence of God – even in the deepest, darkest places. Elie Wiesel said, 'Memory is a passion no less powerful or pervasive than love.' Indeed, memories should serve to recall the past and *change* the future.

CASE STUDY II

Name: *Laura*

Situation: *Thirty-something battling with terminal cancer*

Laura was successful in many ways – a bright girl who studied at Oxford University and went on to have a high-flying career in sales and marketing. She had become a Christian before going to university, and seemed sorted in her beliefs. Her faith was based on believing what the Bible says about human nature and understanding how this applied directly to her own life. 'As I came to understand a little more of God's character, the worst thing was realizing quite how that applied to me ... the Bible was teaching me the truth about what I was like, and [that] I couldn't change my heart.' She came to realize that she couldn't change her heart, but *God* could. Laura's decision to follow and trust in Jesus Christ was tested intellectually during her time at Oxford: 'University was such a challenge to my faith as students do talk about ideas and are really willing to challenge your faith ... Time and again I found myself trying to show my friends that there was historical evidence for Christ's existence and for him being who he said he was – God himself, who was made man.'

This confidence was to be tested in a poignant way a few years later when she was struck by a brain haemorrhage during a meeting at work. She found herself in hospital awaiting a major operation, with the possibility of facing brain damage, or death. 'As I lay there in the hospital, I knew God had me in his hands, and no matter what happened in the operation, whether I woke up or not, I was safe. I knew he had promised me life after death, and that I would go on somewhere better. That feeling of incredible security and peace was amazing. I remember at the time I was calling people and saying goodbye to them. My poor friends had just heard about what had happened, and on the phone I was saying, "I'm going to be okay, I'm in God's hands whatever happens." I think I upset a few friends!'

Laura came round from the operation and all was well. She felt God had given her an amazing gift of life, and she wanted to use it by spending most of her time helping Christian students to grow in their faith and understanding of God and the Bible, and to tell others about Jesus Christ.

Six years later, though, she was again confronted with major health issues. She was diagnosed with skin cancer. At first the doctors couldn't give an accurate prognosis, but as time progressed the cancer spread and it was later confirmed that

Laura had tumours in both her lungs. Almost two years after first discovering the skin cancer, she said, 'Although I looked perfectly healthy I was dying. It is just taking a lot longer for me to die than we originally thought, which I'm glad about. Obviously I had to think very hard about what I believed and whether it was true.'

It is quite rare to die of cancer in your thirties. Laura reflected, 'God helped me in a number of ways to cope with dying at a relatively young age. There are promises in [the Bible] about death. Jesus Christ said that he came to die. Once he was talking to some women who had just lost their brother. He had been dead and buried in a tomb for four days. He was also a good friend of Jesus. The comfort he gives these women is a bit strange. He said: "I am the resurrection and the life. He who believes in me will live, even though he dies; and whoever lives and believes in me will never die. Do you believe this?"[10] This is a man claiming that he has the whole key to life and death wrapped up in his very self, and then just to prove it he gave just one command and his friend Lazarus came out of the tomb after being dead for four days.

'This was recorded by eyewitnesses. Then Jesus went on to die himself and rose from the dead. For me this is the real guarantee that there is life after death. Jesus rose from the dead, [and therefore] he has been through death ahead of me. I do not have to fear death. God has promised that for those who love him, there is a life to come that Christ knows about and he is there. That life has none of the tears and the hurt and the things that we do to one another that ruin this world; it's a perfect world. That for me was an incredible comfort. I know that at the end of [life], there is something better to come, which has really kept me going. [God] has given me promises for my death.'

Laura also found that God had given her promises for life. The experience of the brain haemorrhage had changed her attitude: 'I knew that feeling of peace and security was supernatural. I haven't ever been worried about death since that, and I think that has been quite a help for this and for coping with cancer.'

God's promise to stay with his people was also a source of hope for Laura. Many years ago God said, 'The LORD himself goes before you and will be with you; he will never leave you nor forsake you. Do not be afraid; do not be discouraged.'[11] In Laura's own words: 'That's certainly true in my life. Every morning I wake up and I don't know if another symptom will show itself, or that it will be the day I go to hospital and hear more bad news. The hardest thing about all this has been my having to tell my family and friends more and more bad news. So every day you get up and you can't step outside your body and go on a holiday and forget about the fact that you are ill. You have to live with it. I have just been so amazed at how God has stepped in every time I've asked for help and said I can't cope with this. As I've cried out to him and said, "Today is going to be a real struggle, God," he has stepped in and has kept me so calm, and so at peace, and so joyful.

'I can truly say that I haven't had a day of despair since this cancer was diagnosed and further diagnosis revealed I'm dying. I've had hard times and shocking news. I've had really difficult phone conversations and times with family and friends. But God has been there in all of it and kept me calm and at peace. And I've never really asked the question, "Why?" It's just been incredible to [experience] the love of a God who can keep us calm and happy in what have been quite difficult circumstances. He has given me hope for the future in my death, but he has also provided incredible support in my life, which has been amazing. Again, I have to say it is only supernatural, because I'm certainly not a calm person normally. It has actually been amazing to experience it.'

To crowds of students at Cambridge University about ten months before she died, Laura said, 'When you face death, I want you to know there is something good to go on to. You can die with confidence in the arms of a loving Father, knowing you are safe and that you are his child. It has been great living out my life as a child of God. It has been wonderful – the best part of my life! I want you to know, like I do, that whatever happens to you tomorrow, you are secure. You can know that God loves you; that nothing can happen that he can't protect you from and keep you safe throughout.'

9. FORGIVENESS

In the course of life, there will inevitably be incidents when each individual is challenged to forgive, as well as to ask for forgiveness. Petty incidents may be easier to deal with, but where the hurt cuts deep, the need to forgive is even more acute, and it can seem an impossible task. As Oxford and Cambridge scholar and author C. S. Lewis put it, 'Everyone says forgiveness is a lovely idea, until they have something to forgive.'[1] And yet, the challenge for us is to do what God commands, and what he has demonstrated, namely to forgive. We are used to living by rules and regulations, but Christ teaches that life is to be lived by *love*, not law, by *principles*, not rules. When a person becomes a Christian, the Holy Spirit – God himself – comes to live inside them. He gives the ability and strength to do what otherwise would be impossible. So, with the power and help of the Holy Spirit, a Christian is able to forgive, even in the most difficult of circumstances.

Learning forgiveness

Jesus was asked by his disciple Peter how many times a person should forgive another. Peter then suggested that the answer was seven. Jesus replied that seven was not sufficient, and seventy times seven was more like it. While he quoted a certain and definite number, he was using a linguistic device to mean an uncertain and indefinite number: we are to forgive infinitely. He then told a parable to explain the basis for our beliefs and behaviour.

The story was of a servant who owed his master a fortune, but when he couldn't pay, he begged for and received mercy. The master cancelled his debt. This forgiven man then tracked down a fellow servant who owed him a tiny amount in comparison with the debt he had just had cancelled. Instead of listening to the pleas for mercy from his fellow servant, however, the forgiven servant had his debtor thrown in prison. When the master heard the story of such callous treatment, he went to the servant, rebuked him, revoked the clearing of the debt, and had him thrown in prison until he could pay.[2]

The lessons are clear: all that every Christian has, namely forgiveness, peace with God and an eternal relationship with him, is entirely due to the grace and goodness of God. In turn, gratitude should be the basis of the Christian's behaviour. Because God has forgiven us so much, we in turn should forgive others. Whatever they have done to us, it is no match for the way we have disregarded and rebelled against God. God has shown to Christians both mercy (not getting what we do deserve) and grace (getting what we do not deserve). If a person does not know God as a forgiving God, he or she will never know him as the Father God. The responsibility for those who have been forgiven is that they will forgive others.

Demonstrating grace

Demonstrating to others what she herself had received from God was what motivated Jo Pollard, whose husband Michael was murdered in Hungary in 1997. For thirty years Michael and Jo, with their family, had taken humanitarian aid, medication, Bibles and Christian books into Communist Europe. They had experienced amazing answers to prayer, both in crossing the borders into the Communist bloc and travelling throughout those 'closed' countries.

Eight years after the 'Iron Curtain' had collapsed, when they were on their way to the Ukraine with desperately needed provisions, they were robbed in a lay-by. Michael was bludgeoned to death and an attempt was made on Jo's life.

Three teenagers were later found guilty of murder, but from a hospital bed in Hungary to the ITV News in the UK, Jo said she bore no malice. At Michael's funeral she even sang as a solo the hymn 'How great Thou art'. She regularly prayed for the three men who had killed her husband. Later she visited the jail in Hungary where the men were held. Two of the three prisoners were willing to meet her in the prison, where she told them that she forgave them and presented them with small gifts. One of them has subsequently asked Christ for forgiveness.[3]

To forgive was no mean task. Jo not only lost her husband and the father of her three children, but she has also suffered serious ill health since the attack. Jo was not minimizing what had happened, but recognized that she too had received forgiveness, and now she could show it to these men.

Avoiding bitterness

Repeatedly, the Bible teaches that Christians should forgive. Jesus said, 'Blessed are the merciful, for they will be shown mercy.'[4] The 'Lord's Prayer' – Jesus' model prayer – says,

'Forgive us our sins, for we also forgive everyone who sins against us.'[5] Even on the cross, Jesus prayed to his Father that there would be forgiveness for those responsible for his execution: 'Father, forgive them, for they do not know what they are doing.'[6] And the apostle Paul wrote to Christians in the church in Ephesus, 'Be kind and compassionate to one another, forgiving each other, just as in Christ God forgave you.'[7]

To forgive others is to do what we most want God to do for us. In being willing to receive God's forgiveness and willing to forgive others, it is right to forgive ourselves as well, otherwise we are setting ourselves as a higher judge than God himself. Inability to forgive ourselves is often based on the fear that we will commit the same sin again. The Holy Spirit can give us the strength to overcome the things that dog us. As we learn to forgive ourselves, we consequently live at peace with ourselves even though we are conscious of past failures.

> *To forgive others is to do what we most want God to do for us.*

To forgive and be forgiven is therapeutic. In contrast, to hold bitterness or resentment, to seek vengeance or bear malice wears away at our innermost being, distorting the image of joy and peace that one can see sometimes in a toddler or a young person. Better to forgive and let God avenge the wrong. He is merciful, but absolutely just, so there are some things that are best left in his hands.

We can have confidence that God, who instructs us to forgive, will give us the strength to do what may appear impossible if we are willing to do what he commands. It was said of the sixteenth-century Archbishop Cranmer that if you did him an injury, he was sure to be your friend. Clearly he had cultivated obedience to Jesus' command to love our enemies and pray for those who persecute us.

Bitterness is dealt with by resetting our expectations. Giving our rights over to God deals a death-blow to bitterness which can spring up within. For example, a cancer patient becomes bitter because he feels he has a right to good health. If instead he gave that right to God, by praying and saying, 'Whether or not I have good health is in your hands,' then he can find rest whatever lies ahead; he is accepting God's purpose for his life and can therefore be thankful rather than bitter. So Joseph, whose 'coat of many colours' was taken from him as he was sold into slavery by his brothers, could later say to them, 'You intended to harm me, but God intended it for good . . .'[8]

CASE STUDY III
Names: *John and Lisa*
Situation: *Married couple who lost their daughter in the terrorist attack on Pan-Am Flight 103, which exploded over Lockerbie, Scotland*

John and Lisa Mosey will never forget Christmas 1988. It has become the pivot of their lives; the point which separates all the events and memories. As John turned on the TV to catch the news on the evening of 21 December, his immediate emotion was sympathy for the passengers and crew of a plane that had crashed over a small Scottish town. Sixteen-year-old Marcus was sitting on the sofa, and Lisa and John were perched on the arm. 'How awful – the poor people!' they remember one of them saying. Then the news reporter continued with the details. 'Pan-Am Flight 103, flying from London to New York, exploded above the Scottish border at about three minutes past seven, raining its debris down on this little town of Lockerbie.'

'That's Helga's flight!' burst from Lisa's lips. John had returned from driving their nineteen-year-old daughter to Heathrow airport from their home near Birmingham only a few hours earlier. The possibility of such a thing happening to her just hadn't crossed his mind. 'These things happen to others; they never happen to me.' Like many of us, he was used to being just an observer of other people's tragedies. There followed a stunned silence as the unthinkable slowly expanded, filling not only their minds but every nerve and cell of their bodies.

'No! No! No! No!' broke the silence as Marcus screamed at the screen. The solitary word 'Helga...' quietly, almost silently, managed to escape from somewhere deep down inside Lisa. John stood as if dumb, his tongue unable to articulate. The news flash ended and the news report moved on to other, seemingly trivial matters, such as how many millions of pounds were being spent that Christmas using credit cards, the sports results and the weather forecast.

Helga was a talented musician, accomplished on the piano, recorder and violin, but her real passion was singing. Her mezzo-soprano voice was in demand. She sang with one of the country's leading Bach choirs and was selected from all the schools in Britain to sing in the National Youth Choir. Her ambition was to sing professionally and a music professor at Lancaster University, where she had secured a place to study music, said that he had little doubt that she would have made her mark on the music world.

They switched off the TV. John remembers saying something about asking God to help them. Then the three of them stood together in the middle of the room with their arms around each other as they lifted up their broken and perplexed hearts to God in prayer. Now, years later, they say with certainty that God has certainly helped them. That life-changing Christmas was the beginning of a journey which they never wanted, but which has never ceased to amaze them.

Within minutes the doorbell and telephone were ringing. In the three hours before midnight over forty people came to them to share their grief. Some stayed just a few silent minutes, some prayed with them and tried to encourage them, others fell apart emotionally and the Moseys had to help them! 'This support continued for several weeks,' recalls John, 'making us glad that we were part of such a very real church family. For weeks, each morning after breakfast we would open ten to twenty envelopes which the bewildered postman had delivered. The messages that helped us most seemed to be the ones that made us cry.'

By the evening after the disaster they realized that they were going to be a focus for media attention. A TV news team arrived at the Mosey home and asked if they could interview them. One of the questions they were asked was 'Has this destroyed your faith?' 'Well,' John replied, 'this is where we prove whether what we have preached and said we believed for most of our lives is real, or whether it is just a game.' John and Lisa now say that during the years since Helga's death they have found the grace and love of God, and the strength that he gives, to be *more* real than they had ever previously experienced.

It wasn't until five days after the disaster that John was able to begin properly to formulate his strategy for surviving this dreadful blow to their family. At five o'clock in the morning he sat at Helga's desk in her room at the top of their house. Nothing could alter the dreadful facts. The cry for revenge towards the terrorists was already being heard from some of the victims' relatives. John certainly agreed that the guilty parties should be brought to justice to deter others of similar mind, but he felt he could not seek personal revenge, even against those who had so cruelly murdered his nineteen-year-old daughter.

He cried to God, 'Lord, I can't be like that.' John saw that if he sought revenge against his enemies, he reduced himself to their level and gave the devil 100% interest on his investment in evil men's lives. 'No,' he decided, 'our anger must be directed, not against the small fry who plant bombs, but against the arch-terrorist, the force behind all the world's evils, Satan himself.' His mind went to the apostle Paul's letter to the Romans in the Bible: 'Do not be overcome by evil, but overcome evil with good.'[9]

In the weeks following Christmas, friends set up the 'Helga Mosey Memorial Trust' for the care and education of needy children in the Third World. A beautiful home in the Philippines has been built for abandoned and abused children. When John and Lisa visit there and see those healthy and loved children, knowing that many of them would be dead today if Helga was alive, they feel that they have given something back.

John, a church minister, had prepared his Christmas Day sermon some days before Helga's death. As he stood to deliver it on Christmas morning, it dawned on him how apt it was. It was entitled 'The Empty Chair in Heaven'. He had decided to preach from the Bible verse 'when the time had fully come, God sent his Son'.[10] With tears in his eyes he spoke about how God the Father gave up, in a sense, the immediate relationship of his Son for thirty-three years. The temporary parting with their daughter and the empty chair in their home gave John some sense of relating, in human terms, to God's situation.

On Christmas Day 1988 the Moseys followed their usual routine, but with little appetite and heavy hearts. They missed Helga's laugh, her help in the kitchen, her music. Their presents to her had been in her suitcase. She had left gifts at home for each of them. Marcus handed round the beautifully wrapped packages. 'To Dad, with love from Helga and Marcus': a pair of gloves, almost too precious to wear. The family sat quietly, desperately holding the last tangible expressions of her love for them.

They will never forget that Christmas. They remember the shock and the numbness as they did their best to cope. They recall the ache in their hearts and the physical pain of their loss. But they also remember the love and thoughtfulness of friends, neighbours and even complete strangers and the warm support of their great Christian family. They think too of the overwhelming assurance that, although they did not understand why God had allowed this to happen, and they certainly didn't like it, somehow he knew all about it and they could trust him.

Less than a year later someone said to Lisa, 'Haven't you got over it yet?' John later explained, 'The loss of someone whom you love very much isn't like an illness you get over. It is more like an amputation which you learn to live with. We will feel the loss for the rest of our lives, but with God's help we might just become better people for it.'

10. COMPASSION

The greatest world atrocity to have happened to date in my lifetime was the 1994 genocide in Rwanda. In the short space of 100 days, one-tenth of the population of that African state were massacred. Deep-seated hatred between the Hutus and Tutsis ran riot as national radio whipped up support for the Hutu rebels, precipitating a mass murder of the Tutsis and the deaths of many fighters on both sides.

The film *Hotel Rwanda* tells the true story of Paul Rusesabagina, manager of the prestigious Hotel des Mille Collines in Kigali. A Hutu himself, he had married a Tutsi. During the uprising he used his position in the hotel, and his Hutu status, to shelter 1,268 Tutsis from the savage killings taking place outside the hotel grounds. The film not only captures the intense psychological terror of the genocide and the inability – or unwillingness – of the world's powers to intervene, but also one man's reaction to the horrors, evil and injustice around him. In times like this, individuals can demonstrate extraordinary strength and courage to stand up for and shelter the needy. Yet Christians in all situations are called on to step out of their comfort zones, to respond to injustice and to show compassion.

Responding to injustice

In First World countries it is comparatively easy for Christians to hold strong beliefs and to focus on our own needs, while ignoring the plight of millions living on the same planet. In Europe, where we appear to lack for nothing, Christians focus their efforts too easily on the inconsequential inconveniences of living for Jesus, rather than taking notice of the plight of millions on the other side of the Mediterranean Sea. Social concerns of Christians in the USA largely focus on moral-social-ethical issues such as abortion and homosexuality. Although they may be worthy causes, one cannot help but think that their concerns are out of balance, as they campaign for these issues from a position of economic comfort in leafy suburbs while almost 10% of their neighbours in Latin America live below the poverty line.[1]

One of the great transformations to take place when people truly come to know Jesus Christ personally is that their view of the world is altered. They become part of a global family, with 'brothers and sisters' around the globe. A nomadic family living in northern Mongolia, single people working in the financial districts of Tokyo, New York, London and Sydney, a remote tribe in the jungle of Papua New Guinea, and a young couple trying to survive in a shanty town in Honduras can all be united as followers of Jesus Christ and part of his worldwide family, the church.

This principle is illustrated from troubled regions in Africa. The Hutu and Tutsi conflict that ravaged Rwanda also engulfed other African countries during the mid-1990s, including Burundi. Fighting broke out on the university campus, and a number of Hutu students were killed; others fled to nearby mountains. They were followed by Tutsi Christians, who took food and clothing first to their Christian 'brothers and sisters', but also to others. Some of these Tutsi students were later rejected by their families because they put their allegiance to fellow believers in Jesus Christ ahead of tribal allegiance. However, the principal of the university, who did not call himself a Christian, said on record, 'Our culture is disintegrating. On our campus there are three types of people: Hutus, Tutsis, and Christians. If our culture is to survive, we must follow the examples of the Christians.'[2]

One of the characteristics of this worldwide church 'family' is that Christians have a desire, and a responsibility, to care for their spiritual brothers and sisters who are in need. This might involve making the effort to talk to a fellow Christian even if they are not their 'type', or caring for someone recently widowed, or providing meals for students at church to save them from yet another beans-on-toast or pasta salad. It might, on the other hand, mean giving a few weeks, months, or even years to offer practical and spiritual support to Christian 'brothers' and 'sisters' in Uganda, Afghanistan, Lima, or inner-city Birmingham or Glasgow.

Showing compassion

Belief that God is ultimately good and in control does not mean that Christians can sit back and relax. The Old Testament prophets had denounced the ungodliness of nations which neglected the needs of orphans, widows, immigrants and the poor. The prophet Micah said:

[God] has showed you, O man, what is good.
  And what does the LORD require of you?
To act justly and to love mercy
  and to walk humbly with your God.[3]

Jesus himself was moved with compassion when he saw people who were like 'sheep without a shepherd'.[4] He healed the sick, giving sight to the blind, hearing to the deaf, speech to the mute, strength to the lame and paralysed, and even life to the dead. He fed hungry crowds, cured people with leprosy, cast out demons from the tormented, and met the spiritual needs of those who came to him. He worked and taught, and trained his disciples to do the same. He went about doing good. He cared for the underdogs, the neglected, the needy, and took time with those ignored by others.

His followers have sought to follow his example. Early in church history Christians sold what they had and distributed their goods to the poor. Collections were taken to give to the poor and people who had suffered because of famine. Jesus' disciple John wrote to Christians saying, 'If anyone has material possessions and sees his brother in need but has no pity on him, how can the love of God be in him? Dear children, let us not love with words or tongue but with actions and in truth.'[5]

Followers of Christ experience an inner compulsion to hard work, in physical, social and spiritual ways. And the Bible commands it too. For example, during the period of social reform in the eighteenth century it was the evangelical community that worked for the abolition of slavery, child labour and prison abuses. Christians have been at the forefront of establishing schools and health care and hospitals throughout the world. Others have given their lives to guarantee free speech, to alleviate suffering and to proclaim the message of Jesus, who said that he had come 'to preach good news to the poor ... to proclaim freedom for the prisoners and recovery of sight for the blind, to release the oppressed...'[6]

I admire Nelson Mandela's lack of bitterness, and the selfless leadership he showed upon his release from prison. In his autobiography he recalls a touching incident which happened in the dark years, as he calls them, of his time in jail on Robben Island:

> During this time I experienced another grievous loss. One cold morning in July of 1969, three months after I learned of Winnie's incarceration, I was called to the main office on Robben Island and handed a telegram. It was from my youngest son, Makgatho, and it was only a sentence long. He informed me that his older brother, my first and oldest son, Madiba Thembekile, whom we called Thembi, had been killed in a motorcar accident in the Transkei. Thembi was then twenty-five years old, and the father of two small children.

Compassion should be a hallmark of Christians, and we can learn much from the example of Jesus, as well as individuals like Walter in South Africa and Paul Rusesabagina of Hotel Rwanda.

> What can I say about such a tragedy? I was overwrought about my wife, I was still grieving for my mother, and then to hear such news ... I do not have words to express the sorrow, or the loss I felt. It left a hole in my heart that can never be filled.
>
> I returned to my cell and lay on my bed. I do not know how long I stayed there, but I did not emerge for dinner. Some of the men looked in, but I said nothing. Finally, Walter came to me

and knelt beside my bed, and I handed him the telegram. He said nothing, but only held my hand. I do not know how long he remained with me. There is nothing one man can say to another at such a time.[7]

I admire the silent compassion that Walter demonstrated in that prison cell towards a man who seemed to have lost everything. It reminds me of Jesus freely touching ostracized lepers, or his tender words to an unrecognized widow who generously gave money that others would have discarded. Compassion should be a hallmark of Christians, and we can learn much from the example of Jesus, as well as individuals like Walter in South Africa and Paul Rusesabagina of *Hotel Rwanda*.

CASE STUDY IV
Name: *Roger Carswell*
Situation: *An experience of depression*

I am not a doctor, psychologist or psychiatrist, but I have been a patient. What I share here is simply one person's journey with depression. What I have been through is a common enough experience, and though it has been terrible, I am aware of many who have endured much more serious times of suffering.

Personal experience
I have always regarded myself as a fairly cheerful and at times mischievous character. However, I was just sixteen years old when depression started to trouble me. I am drawn to melancholic music, books and paintings. From my teenage years I have been an intermittent insomniac. I work late into the night, but then find it difficult to sleep. I love my work, and can be a

workaholic. I don't find it easy to 'switch off' or rest, and rarely have a break. I can be a sensitive soul, feeling deeply for the hurts of others, and I don't easily shake off the thoughts of what others are suffering. I take these things to heart and they remain there, gnawing away at me.

When this particular bout started, I began to find certain aspects of my work overwhelming. Every phone call seemed too much for me, and I couldn't cope with inconsequential chatter, or even the laughter of others. I became annoyed even when people asked me to speak somewhere (which is my beloved life's work!), wishing rather to be left alone. I was walking an emotional tightrope, and finding myself easily falling off and plunging into the safety net of tears and sobbing. Yet I couldn't put a finger on the reason why.

A doctor friend advised me to take a sabbatical, and so I took a four-month break. Looking back, that period became sick leave rather than a sabbatical. My state of mind had deteriorated. I was beginning to sink into a depth of great, inward darkness. I continued to read the Bible, pray and go to church, but avoided talking with people.

My mind was telling me things that were not true. The depression affected my perception of things, so that I had a distorted point of view. For some time I had thought I would collapse while preaching in the pulpit. I believed nobody cared whether I lived or died. I went to bed each evening hoping I would die in the night, and would wake up the next day feeling I could not face the hours ahead. However, even in my lowest moments I was convinced that God was in control of all that was going on, and that he would not waste any experience I was having. I am aware that others struggle with doubts, which compound their suffering.

I was encouraged to see a professional counsellor, but I did not want to talk to anyone else. To suffer alone was itself too much for me, without the added burden of speaking to someone I did not know. Every conversation added to the inward pain and hurt. I felt that any meaningful explanation of the complexities of my mind and life would demand of me more than I felt able to give.

Many people wrote or sent cards assuring me of their prayers, each of which was appreciated. Two friends in particular wrote at length, and one (helpfully) insisted on visiting me. Both assured me that I would eventually come through the depression. Although I felt there was no future, the fact that two people wrote the same thing, giving a more positive view of the future, was very encouraging. I had yet to learn that today is not for ever. I have reread those letters many times and they have proved to be a repeated source of encouragement.

I remember how on one occasion my son simply put his arm around me when he found me crying in my study. It was a moment of great comfort to me. Being hugged is part of being healed.

Suicide

Although I don't generally drink alcohol, in the darkness of my depression I wanted to get drunk. I thought that if I was drunk, at least for an evening, I would not feel the tangible, emotional pain that was within. That pain is just as real as toothache. It makes darkness more preferable to light. As a friend of mine wrote to me, 'It gives the impression that "the sun is laughing at you".' This pain can deprive us of pleasures that we formerly took for granted. Time and again I have empathized with the last words of Vincent Van Gogh, 'La tristesse durera', which means, 'The sadness will never go away.'

Thoughts of dying dominated my mind. I craved death. I knew that suicide is always wrong; it is not natural, and it is a breaking of God's commandment, for God who is the giver of

life says we are not to take life, even our own; it is self-murder.
In addition, it transfers the pain to the innocent family members
who are left. But I knew also that it is not an unforgivable sin,
and at one particularly low time I meticulously planned my
'accidental death'. I planned a suicide that I was sure would be
recorded as accidental death. I cannot tell you how near I was to
taking my own life, but I refrained from doing so, because I felt
it would scar the lives of my wife and four children until their
dying day.

The book of Psalms was a great blessing to me. Repeatedly I
found that the psalmist had experienced just what I was feeling.
He reminds himself of God's blessings in the past and his
promises for the future. Psalms 42 and 43 are good examples of
this. But there are many other examples where the psalmist
imaginatively describes his troubles as waves of sorrow which
were overtaking him. In the Psalms, I read of anger, disappointment, the sense of being let down, frustration – but also of joy,
relief and wonderment. When times were very dark, it was
good to be able to assure myself that 'God is going to get
me through this' and that, with his help, I can even glorify God
through this experience.

Recovery

With the passage of many months I was beginning to recover. I
was back at work, speaking publicly and mixing with others,
but I was still struggling. One day, while I was having a meal
with a pastor, I again began to cry. He recommended that I go
to see a Christian psychiatrist he knew of in London, which I
did. I remember so clearly the psychiatrist saying that I was sick,
but that he could help me.

This promise of help meant the world to me. I had already
tried three different types of drugs. Two proved to be of no help,
the other did strange things to my mind and foolishly I stopped

taking it abruptly. This caused further traumas to my mind. The psychiatrist put me on an older type of drug, and gradually this seemed to work as it drew me out of my depression.

Eventually ... slowly ... erratically ... I came out of that dreadful bout of depression. I still need to learn to be patient with myself, and try to understand what was happening to me, as recovery is very gradual.

Suffering and glory

In 1 Peter and elsewhere in the Bible, we read that suffering characterizes the Christian life. Christians are not immune to normal sicknesses. However, we can be sure that God does not forget us in any situation, and he is well able to heal – if that is his purpose. God never wastes any tears. He never wastes any pain. And we can trust that he will use what we experience for good.

So, what have I learnt through this period?

I have learnt afresh to trust God in the darkness. Because my mind was telling me things that were not true, I consciously reminded myself of what I know to be true. This is what the psalmist does in Psalm 42. For example, in verses 5 to 6 we read:

> Why are you downcast, O my soul?
>   Why so disturbed within me?
> Put your hope in God,
>   for I will yet praise him,
>   my Saviour and my God.[8]

The psalmist spoke truth to his soul, and questioned its disturbed state. I had to remind myself of God's love towards me, of how he has blessed and helped me in the past, and of what he promises in the future. It was good to know that Jesus, who himself was called 'a man of sorrows',[9] cared and could cope.

In Isaiah 45 we read that God says:

I will give you the treasures of darkness,
   riches stored in secret places,
so that you may know that I am the LORD,
   the God of Israel, who summons you by name.[10]

In the darkness and despair of depression, as I felt I was sinking ever deeper, God gave me treasures. I experienced God's love and tender, therapeutic care. I am certainly aware of my own vulnerability in a way I had not recognized before, and I believe I have a more compassionate view towards those who suffer mental illness; before, I was quite dispassionate towards mental weakness. This was an important thing for me to learn, because as Christians we should have compassion on those whose physical and mental strength has collapsed. There is no stigma in having mental illness such as depression. There is no blame attached, just as there is none to someone suffering from flu or tuberculosis.

I am aware that my depression could recur. Frankly, I would fear it happening and would not wish the inward darkness on anyone, but I am also aware that God works all things together for my good and his glory. He is God and he is in control, and whatever the future holds, God can renew and keep me.

11. ACCEPTANCE

Pain is not always dramatic or headline hitting. It might even be something one suffers alone; a hurt one carries around that is too painful to share with others. Loneliness, fear, poor self-image and rejection can hurt deep and sharp, and it's easy to think that no-one cares or understands.

American lyricist and singer Janis Ian captured the sentiments of many in her hit single 'At Seventeen':

> To those of us who knew the pain
> Of valentines that never came
> And those whose names were never called
> When choosing sides for basketball
> It was long ago and far away
> The world was younger than today
> When dreams were all they gave for free
> To ugly duckling girls like me.

We all play the game, and when we dare
We cheat ourselves at solitaire
Inventing lovers on the phone
Repenting other lives unknown
That call and say – come on, dance with me
And murmur vague obscenities
At ugly girls like me, at seventeen.[1]

Being imperfect in a 'perfect' world

We live in a fallen, broken world which is obsessed with an unspoiled, perfect image. Whether it is finances, looks, career, relationships, intelligence, holidays, property, cars or talent, our world is consumed by success. Values are being squeezed out of society, and image is all that matters. If you don't make the grade, you're out; this world has no place for losers.

But wait! Whose world is this? Who rules the world? Does the world really belong to the rich and famous or to the powerful politicians? Do the media *really* control the direction this world is taking? It's easy to believe the answer to these questions is a resounding 'yes'. The reality, though, is that the true ruler of the world isn't swung by the size of one's wallet, or by the number of letters after one's name. The true ruler of the world loves 'ugly duckling girls' as much as those on the front of celebrity magazines. He is not ageist, sexist or racist, but loves each person on this earth – past, present and future – as his own. He longs for each one to be reconciled to himself. This isn't a throwaway line. He sent his only Son, so that each person on earth could be rescued and brought into relationship with him – a relationship that is based on us not being perfect, on us not deserving anything, but in return being made 'perfect' and receiving everything. God, the ruler of the earth, longs to be with the lonely, to calm the fearful, to embrace those with low self-esteem and to welcome the rejected. He has promised his companionship, and we can be sure that he will guide, guard and satisfy in a way that nothing or no-one else can.

Living with fear

Memories of the past so often haunt people, but then thoughts of the future sometimes do the same. We can harbour a deep-seated fear that there will never again be happiness, companionship or purpose to life. We can do nothing about the past, and even the future is largely out of our control, but we can adjust our attitudes to today, with transforming effects. Jesus addressed this issue when he said:

> ... do not worry about your life, what you will eat or drink; or about your body, what you will wear. Is not life more important than food, and the body more important than clothes? Look at the birds of the air; they do not sow or reap or store away in barns, and yet your heavenly Father feeds them. Are you not much more valuable than they? Who of you by worrying can add a single hour to his life?
>
> And why do you worry about clothes? See how the lilies of the field grow. They do not labour or spin. Yet I tell you that not even Solomon in all his splendour was dressed like one of these ... So do not worry, saying, 'What shall we eat?' or 'What shall we drink?' or 'What shall we wear?' ... But seek first his [God's] kingdom and his righteousness, and all these things will be given to you as well. Therefore do not worry about tomorrow, for tomorrow will worry about itself. Each day has enough trouble of its own.[2]

Worry is like a fog – millions of minute globules of water dim our vision of the way ahead. Worry is useless, needless and godless if instead we can have a trust in God that leaves us confident in his purposes. I have found that worry can be overcome. This comes about through recognizing that we cannot deal with the issues, but that we can give our concerns to God and leave them with him. If the worry continues to nag away, we remind ourselves that God is dealing with the problem. This means practising what we read in the Psalms: 'Cast your cares on the LORD and he will sustain you.'[3]

Finding strength

C. S. Lewis expressed wryly the common Christian attitude in one of his letters: 'We are not necessarily doubting that God will do the best for us; we are wondering how painful the best will turn out to be.'[4] This is certainly true when facing death. We know our future after death is certain, but before this we may go through a terrible time of pain and suffering.

Sometimes, the weight of the world and life's difficulties can be so heavy that we cannot imagine a way of making it through without crumbling. However, the Creator God loves us and gives hope to those who put their confidence in him. Suffering is so draining, but God's strength is eternal and it is there to be tapped. Isaiah, a prophet who lived around 700 BC, wrote some words which were famously read by Eric Liddell's character in *Chariots of Fire*:

> The LORD is the everlasting God,
>   the Creator of the ends of the earth.
> He will not grow tired or weary,
>   and his understanding no-one can fathom.
> He gives strength to the weary
>   and increases the power of the weak.

Even youths grow tired and weary,
   and young men stumble and fall;
but those who hope in the LORD
   will renew their strength.
They will soar on wings like eagles;
   they will run and not grow weary,
   they will walk and not be faint.[5]

While our bodies may fail, our spirits be crushed and our minds falter, we can find new sources of energy and strength in God. He can give us the resources we need, not necessarily to escape the circumstances we are in, but to cope, and even to 'soar' in situations where we felt we were sinking.

Accepting unknowns

I have often heard people talk about faith in a mystical way, particularly when it comes to suffering. For example, someone shares that they have terminal cancer, and they receive the reply, 'Well, it's a good thing you have faith.' Or a person dies, and friends say, 'At least they had a strong faith.' What is wrong about this view of 'faith' is that it sees it as a magic charm or a good luck mascot. In reality, the most important aspect of faith is the *focus* of the faith – who or what the faith is in. Misplaced faith is as good as no faith at all.

Faith in God is based on the truth of who he is and how he has demonstrated himself. It is not a 'blind faith', but a faith based on facts and experience. We don't know everything about God, as his very nature as God means we cannot possibly understand everything about him. However, we can trust in his character and his promises. As we witness how he has demonstrated himself in the past and how he has worked in our own lives, we can learn to trust him for the unknowns.

We don't always know if we will be healed from an illness, rescued from death, enjoy long-lasting relationships, keep our job, be free from natural disaster, or have enough resources to live on; yet we can trust that God is in control – of the world and of our own day-to-day lives. He has not left us alone. In fact, he has gone to great lengths to ensure there is a way that we can one day be free of this world and its problems, and enjoy the world as he intended it to be.

I know I often struggle with this as I, like others, prefer to keep 'control'. The idea of submitting ourselves to someone else, even if that 'someone' is God, can be most unappealing. But if we do, we find that the dreaded unknowns can be placed in God's hands and we can rest, assured that he will take care of us – whatever the future holds.

Dr Steve Brady, Principal of a Christian college in England, made a similar point based on Jesus' words, 'You do not realise now what I am doing, but later you will understand.'[6] With a wife suffering from multiple sclerosis and mounting family difficulties, Steve drew three straightforward conclusions from Jesus' words: be glad for what you do know; be humble for what you do not know; and be patient for what you will one day know.[7]

> ... be glad for what you do know; be humble for what you do not know; and be patient for what you will one day know.

Such an attitude in no way excuses a fatalistic approach to life. 'Que sera, sera, whatever will be will be' may have been a hit song in the 1950s, but it is not good theology. We have the role model of Jesus who 'went around doing good',[8] healing the sick and raising the dead, comforting the bereaved and welcoming the outcasts. Like him, Christians should be doing right, striving to better the world around them.

Christians rightly pray for good health. The apostle John wrote to his friend Gaius, saying, 'Dear friend, I pray that you may enjoy good health and that all may go well with you, even as your soul is getting along well.'[9] We pray for protection and help in all situations. The litany in the Anglican Book of Common Prayer includes the following prayer: 'From lightning and tempest; from plague, pestilence, and famine; from battle and murder, and from sudden death, Good Lord, deliver us.'

Christians will work to prevent disaster in this fallen world, and to help the weak and suffering, using legitimate means to bring about social and economic good. The disenfranchised and downtrodden should be able to experience just, economic empowerment and social mobility. The Bible declares that God decries social and economic injustices. After all, he is a just God. Nevertheless, despite our aims, we will always have injustice in this world, because we live in a world that has not yet been put right by the ruler of all, who will one day reign in justice and equity. Coexisting with our striving for justice is the rest in knowing that God, who rules, also overrules in the situations we would naturally avoid at all costs.

CASE STUDY V
Name: *Diane*
Situation: *Young person struggling with chronic pain*

Diane was brought up in the country, and then moved to Leeds to study design. 'I wanted to make it big in the design world, and it was always my goal to be the very best at what I did, even in a very competitive world.' Although her family were Christians, Diane had been far from God for many years. It was following a humanitarian trip to the Ukraine, and while she was working and living in Glasgow, that, as she puts it, 'I met God in a real way.' This changed her life and, from a career perspective, she felt she now wanted to serve God. An opportunity came up for her to be a designer in a Christian organization 'where I could use the gifts and skills he had given me, and give them back to him'. She was in her mid-twenties.

Five months into this new job, Diane started to have a terrible headache – a headache which didn't lift for three months. She kept working through this time, thinking it would be a passing problem. But then her neck and shoulder also began to give her great pain along with the headaches. It was increasingly difficult to hold down a full-time job because the pain was so intense and uncomfortable.

'What was most frustrating was that no-one could put their finger on the cause of the pain.' As a teenager, she had been through the serious, but fairly routine, operation for scoliosis. This involves attaching metal rods to straighten a curved spine. Eleven years later, she started having related problems and went through two years of investigations, treatments, injections, medications and pain clinics before she finally had an operation to relieve her shoulder pain. For three years following this she lived with a low, manageable level of pain in her head, neck and shoulder – all above her metal rods. Unfortunately this improvement was short-lived. Very intense pain started to develop in her lower back – below the rods – and over the course of a year progressed into her legs and feet.

'The fear of another episode of pain-filled days, endless waiting lists, different medications and no real answers to explain the pain set in.' She had been investigating the idea of joining a mission organization and had hopes for this new opportunity, and was devastated that she could no longer pursue this: 'It was the worst thing. I had to accept all over again the reality of the term "chronic pain". The simplest task, such as washing the dishes, was exhausting because the pain was so wearing. Often I would feel that my body was covered in pain from head to foot – quite literally. Bad headaches, neck and shoulder pain, pins and needles in my arms, lower back burning with pain, down my legs and painful feet.'

Looking back on that year, she says, 'It was a year of disappointments, due to a body which constantly let me down. I have a heart to serve God, yet I haven't had the answer I want to my plea which says, "Heal me so I can serve you." Nothing has made sense to me during this time, and I still wonder at what God is doing in my life.' She read God's promise in the Bible that 'in all things God works for the good of those who love him'[10] and asked, 'If that's right, that everything is for his glory, where is the glory he sees in my pain?'

At a particularly low time, when these questions were constantly invading her head, when she couldn't see God in her pain or in her day, she decided 'to pull myself together and seek him. If I couldn't see him, I would have to try and find him. He promised, "You will seek me and find me when you seek me with all your heart."[11] So I went looking.'

At this dramatic turning point, when all seemed quite desperate, Diane sought God and found him in a fresh and real way. 'I saw him most beautifully in creation. I read verses like "I am the Alpha and the Omega, the Beginning and the End"[12] in a new light. I began to look forward to the better things to come, that he has promised; to a time when there will be no pain, when God will wipe every tear.'[13]

And this time, when Diane thought that no doctor could understand her pain and help her, God reminded her of his promise: 'Come to me, all you who are weary and burdened, and I will give you rest.'[14] As she waited on him, he cleared the way for the right doctors to come to light and bring new hope. She still doesn't know the future outcome, but she is awaiting an operation which may or may not work but at least offers a glimmer of hope. 'God has said, "I go before you," and I trust that. He knows the way I take.'

This whole experience has been a huge disappointment to Diane. Big questions remain unanswered: 'Why, when every area of my life is for God – my friendships, my business, my church life – does he not take away my pain? Why, when he has the power to remove it, does he allow so much pain to run riot in my body?' She continues, 'Sometimes we have to live with unanswered questions, but I can't help feeling that I could do so much more without this hindrance in my life. But Jesus suffered, and in all ways is making us more like him, so perhaps this suffering is an honour? Maybe it gives me a taster – and only a taster – of what he went through for me?'

Over the years, Diane has found comfort from the story of Job in the Bible. Job suffered yet he still praised God. 'He suffered and, over time, he got tired and worn down. I know this worn-out feeling. He questioned God, and God replied asking Job who he was to question Almighty God. When I think of this, I am humbled because I realize how mighty God is. I am glad for my suffering at times because it makes me rely more fully on God, who is the maker of all things.'

Without an eternal perspective, Diane acknowledges that she would be without hope. On top of her pain-filled days and her disappointment over her career, her house was devastated by a freak flood in her home city of Carlisle. It has made her focus on the future and see that this world is temporary, and falling apart. 'We have so much better to come in eternity. Even though it is hard at times, we must hold onto the hope that we have in Christ because this world is full of disappointment. The only certainty we have is Christ, and the future he promises to those who trust in him. I know that my future is sealed and I know that, for me, one day I will be free from a body that lets me down. I will be in heaven, with my new body, rejoicing with God – my Creator, and my Deliverer.'

CONCLUSION

Over twenty centuries ago the region of Palestine was rocked by two tragedies. The first was a deliberate act of terrorism, instigated by Pilate and his men, in which a group of Galileans were killed while they worshipped God. In the second incident, eighteen people died when an edifice called the Tower of Siloam collapsed and crushed them. In the same way that we ask the question 'Why?' when we hear of deliberate or accidental tragedies, people put the same question to Jesus two millennia ago. Despite the passage of time, the Bible is always relevant and topical, and we can learn things directly from Jesus' response to these incidents.

We read of these events in the Gospel of Luke.

Now there were some present at that time who told Jesus about the Galileans whose blood Pilate had mixed with their sacrifices. Jesus answered, 'Do you think that these Galileans were worse sinners than all the other Galileans because they suffered this way? I tell you, no! But unless you repent, you too will all perish. Or those eighteen who died when the tower in Siloam fell on them – do you think they were more guilty than all the others living in Jerusalem? I tell you, no! But unless you repent, you too will all perish.'[1]

A desire to talk about disaster and death

We can see that there is often a desire to talk about disaster and death. Although in Britain since the 1960s death has replaced sex as the big taboo subject, there is still an inclination to talk about death and disaster, even if not on a personal level. Following the Boxing Day tsunami in Asia, a friend commented to me that the reaction of friends in London was almost competitive – trying to show who was most 'moved' by what had happened. Although that might be a little cynical, it does show some truth. We love to talk and debate about the tragedies we're witnessing around us. Our news wouldn't be dominated by such dreadful stories if there wasn't appetite for them. In the same way this issue wouldn't have been raised with Jesus had people not wanted to discuss it.

When people are confronted by nationwide troubles, city-wide disaster or suffering closer to home, there is a stirring in hearts and questioning in minds. Often there is an expression, in the best way people are able, of their sympathy and compassion. There is nothing wrong with grief. Jesus wept at the tomb of his friend Lazarus who had died, even though he was to raise back to life this man who had been dead for four whole days. However, places of disaster are often in danger of being turned into 'pagan shrines'. Grief can bring about a mixture of sentiment, superstition and falsehood. Out of desperation for comfort and answers, there can be a tendency to cling onto anything that offers hope, whether true or false.

A need to learn from disasters

We can also see that there is a need to learn from disaster. We want to know if it could have been prevented, and if so who is to blame, and what can be done to avoid such a thing in the future.

Jesus responded to this need, and spoke about the reason for such events. In the case of the murder and martyrdom of the Galilean worshippers, the cause was straightforward: human evil. Pilate's cruelty led to the death of innocent victims. So it was when two planes ploughed into New York's Twin Towers on 11 September 2001, or when the Kurds were gassed and the Marsh Arabs killed by Saddam Hussein's men. The sinfulness of an individual or group led to the suffering and death of hundreds of others.

In contrast, when the Tower of Siloam fell, it was not a specific act of violence, but rather a tragic accident. We are part of the world and all too often caught up in its tragedies. Blame for such incidents cannot be laid at the feet of anybody in particular.

In both cases, Jesus taught that one must not judge people's sins by their present sufferings. The men and women who died were neither more innocent nor more sinful than others. As Jesus also said concerning a man who had been born blind, it was not the sin of the man or his parents that caused his blindness, 'but this happened so that the work of God might be displayed in his life'.[2]

In the discussion about the massacre of the Galileans and the collapse of the Tower of Siloam, Jesus moved the conversation to focus on another lesson we need to learn from disaster and death as he spoke about the need to repent. Twice he said that 'unless you repent, you too will all perish'. C. S. Lewis famously said that God speaks to us through everyday circumstances, but shouts at us through disaster.

John the Baptist, the cousin of Jesus who prepared the way for his coming, had as his great theme 'repent'. Jesus' disciple Peter preached the first 'Christian' sermon. Its theme also was 'repent'. Paul, the man who carried the Christian message throughout the then-known world, continually stressed in his messages the need to 'repent'. Here, too, God himself calls people to 'repent'.

Repentance means a change of heart, mind and ways. It means turning from one's own ways and trusting that these can be completely forgiven because of what Jesus did on the cross. It means accepting God's loving rule and guidance for your life. Repentance is the only way to escape inevitable judgment of our wrongdoing. The Christian faith is not just about belief; it is about a complete transformation.

Jonah, an Old Testament prophet, preached that the city of Nineveh would be destroyed in forty days. All the people in Nineveh repented, and God was merciful to the vast city. The grossly wicked King Manasseh, of whom we read in the Bible, burned his own children as a sacrifice to false gods and led the people of Judah into idolatry and immorality, but he repented and God was merciful even to him.

At the beginning of the eighteenth century, Britain was noted for its debauchery and drunkenness, but through the preaching of an enthusiastic group of evangelists, including John Wesley and George Whitefield, many in Britain experienced a complete transformation, and again God was merciful. This led to great social awareness, and Christian people such as William Wilberforce (who worked for the abolition of slavery), Lord Shaftesbury (who brought about factory and child labour reform), John Howard and Elizabeth Fry (who worked for prison reform) began to campaign tirelessly to alleviate social injustice and suffering.

Today we also need to repent of our sins. It might appear old-fashioned, or completely alien to us, but we all know there are things that are not right in the way we live, think, speak and act. Each of us must turn from sin and renounce it, and turn to Christ asking him to receive us.

A right attitude to develop concerning death and disaster

We see from the incident in Luke 13 that there is a right attitude to develop concerning death and disaster. The 'Troubles' in Northern Ireland were a running sore in the UK in the latter part of the twentieth century. Mingled in with the sadness and tragedy were many incidents of faith and courage. For example, Bill McConnell was the deputy governor of the notorious Maze Prison. He was murdered in front of his wife, Beryl, and three-year-old daughter, Gail.[3]

Bill had a premonition of death three weeks before his murder. He wrote a letter to be read at his funeral. It was also published in national newspapers. The last paragraph read:

> Finally, let no one be alarmed as to my eternal security. In March 1966, I committed my life, talents, work and actions to Almighty God in sure and certain knowledge that however slight my hold upon him may have been during my years at school, university and the prison service, his promises are sure, and his hold on me complete. Nothing can separate me from the love of God in Christ Jesus our Lord.

Do you have such confidence in the face of death? Death is inescapable and, though we never know, it could be sooner than we think. The Tower of Siloam was built for safety, but it proved to be the place of people's death.

Peter Marshall was a greatly respected chaplain to the American Senate. He used to tell this story:

> An old legend tells of a merchant in Baghdad who one day sent his servant to the market. Before very long the servant came back, pale and trembling. In great agitation he said to his master, 'Down in the marketplace I was jostled by a woman in the crowd, and when I turned around I saw it was Death. She looked at me and made a threatening gesture. Master, please lend me your horse, for I must hasten to avoid her. I will ride to Samarra and there I will hide and Death will not find me.'
>
> The merchant lent him his horse and the servant galloped away in great haste. Later the merchant went down to the market and saw Death standing in the crowd. He asked her, 'Why did you frighten my servant this morning? Why did you make a threatening gesture?'
>
> 'That was not a threatening gesture,' Death said. 'It was only a start of surprise. I was astonished to see him in Baghdad, for I have an appointment with him tonight in Samarra!'[4]

Whether our life ends slowly or suddenly, each person will eventually stand before God. It is easy to laugh at the characters who give out Christian leaflets, or hold up banners with Bible sentences or dramatic phrases. However, outside the Hillsborough football ground in Sheffield on the fateful Saturday in April 1989 when ninety-six fans died, Keith Bowers of Morecambe had prayed concerning which banners and leaflets he should carry and hand out to the crowds. The banner he decided on and held up to thousands of football supporters displayed the words 'Prepare to meet your God'. They could not have been more relevant.

A God to trust in preparation for disaster and death

In the passage in Luke 13, we see that there is a God to trust in preparation for possible disaster and certain death. Jesus repeatedly warns us of the vital, urgent need to repent. He is patient, but his warning still applies.

Early in the Bible we read the story of Noah building a giant boat, or ark, before the world's first major catastrophe. For 120 years Noah built and preached to warn the people who worked for him, telling them of impending judgment and letting them know that the ark was the way of escape. Even when the animals and Noah's family had entered the vessel, God kept the ark door open for seven more days. It was a silent sermon and invitation for everyone to enter. We read that eventually God himself shut the door. The time of invitation and the opportunity for the people to repent was over, for ever.

For two thousand years the command to repent and Jesus' invitation, 'Come to me, all you who are weary and burdened, and I will give you rest',[5] has been declared. God will eventually 'close the door' and then it will be too late. 'I tell you,' said Jesus, '... unless you repent, you too will all perish.' Our 'perishing' will be eternal. To be cut off from God in conscious, eternal punishment is a terrible thing. Yet God is compassionate. As the Bible

To be sure of eternal life, we must make sure that our wrongdoing has been forgiven, and that we are in a right relationship with God.

says in John 3:16, 'For God so loved the world that he gave his one and only Son, that whoever believes in him shall not perish but have eternal life.'

Sometimes in funeral services one can get the impression that everyone will go to heaven and be all right after death.

Jesus made it very clear that this is not so. Our sin will keep us out of heaven. To be sure of eternal life, we must make sure that our wrongdoing has been forgiven, and that we are in a right relationship with God.

Christ's death was not an accident. It was God's plan that Jesus should come and lay down his life. It was to be humanity's only hope. Sin always brings death – either the death of the sinner or the death of a substitute. Christ died as the substitute for us. Our sin was laid on him and he took all our guilt so that we might be forgiven. Christ's death was not a disaster; it was the greatest act of love that the world has seen. What looked like a terrible tragedy was actually God demonstrating his great love towards us.

In fact, the death and rising again of the Lord Jesus was God's greatest work. 'God was reconciling the world to himself in Christ, not counting men's sins against them.'[6] Sins committed from the beginning, through the ages to the end of time, were all focused onto Jesus Christ. He was made sin for us. Sin always carries a penalty, but Christ paid for it in our place.

Having died for us, he was buried in a sealed, previously unused tomb in a garden. Three days later Jesus rose from the dead. He overcame the things that overcome us, namely sin and death. Through his death and resurrection, Jesus has opened the way so that we may now be forgiven and enjoy God living in our hearts, minds and lives. As soon as we turn from our own direction and ask Jesus to be our Lord, Saviour and Friend, a relationship with God begins which will last throughout our life and on through eternity.

Time is short, but so are memories. I recently stood at the scene of the fire which tore through a nightclub in Rhode Island in 2003. Ninety-eight people died in the inferno, but the world has largely forgotten this tragedy. In contrast,

Jesus Christ's death has not been forgotten. Significantly, Christians regularly gather in a ceremony where they eat bread and drink a little wine, deliberately remembering that Jesus died for them. Just as the bread is broken to be eaten, so his body was broken. As the wine is sipped, so Jesus' blood was spilt as he died on the cross, to buy for us forgiveness and new life. We can never forget such a sacrifice.

Christ's death is not the last we saw of him. Jesus defeated the grave. He rose again from the dead. Having beaten sin and death, he ascended to heaven and the Bible teaches that one day Jesus will return to be acknowledged as the King of kings and Lord of lords. The oft-repeated prayer, 'Your kingdom come,' will be answered and Christ will establish his reign on earth.

A bigger disaster to avoid

There is a bigger disaster to avoid than the ones that sadly hit the headlines. Perhaps the most tragic word in the English language is the word 'lost'. That is why it is imperative to trust Christ as your Saviour. We each need to answer the question, 'Have I asked Jesus to forgive me and to live within me?'

Will you now ask Christ to forgive your past, guide your present and be with you for ever? There is a degree of urgency about that question. We never know what the future may bring. I wonder whether part of the awfulness of being lost from God is the sense of regret that God was so close, and yet was neglected or refused. In the Old Abbey Kirk at Haddington in Scotland one can read over the grave of Jane Baillie Welsh one of many pathetic and regretful tributes paid by Thomas Carlyle to his neglected wife:

For forty years she was a true and loving helpmate of her husband, and by act and work worthily forwarded me as

none else could . . . She died at London the 21st of April, 1866,
suddenly snatched from him, and the light of his life as if
gone out.

It has been said that the saddest sentence in English literature
is that sentence written by Carlyle in his diary: 'Oh, that I had
you yet for five minutes by my side, that I might tell you all.'

Although Christians cannot answer every question concerning faith in Christ and all that is going on in the world,
they know God, in whom they have believed, and they are
convinced that he will keep them throughout life, through
death and for eternity. The Bible says, 'Everyone who calls
on the name of the Lord will be saved.'[7] There is no need to
have regrets; the offer is open to all.

I would encourage you to pray, to talk to God, and tell
him where you are in your thinking. Share your feelings
about your own personal struggles or troubles in the world.
Ask him to forgive you for all that is wrong, and for not
following him and his ways. Ask him to come to live within
you and, by the power of his Holy Spirit, to be your Lord,
Saviour and Friend. As you trust him like this, ask him to
give you the strength to follow him. Sharing, worshipping
and serving God with other Christians will be of immense
benefit to you as you start to grow in your faith and cultivate
your relationship with God. As you live for him you will find
the privilege of getting to know him here on earth. One day,
in heaven, we will begin to understand better the things that
have puzzled us now.

APPENDIX I : HELPFUL PSALMS

The book of Psalms is the Bible's song book. It is found right in the middle of the Bible and contains 150 psalms which express to God every human emotion. It is impossible to summarize them, but they teach that although life is tough, God is good.

They have been a source of comfort to millions of God's people. Personally, I have repeatedly turned to them and found that they express better than I ever could what is going on in my mind, and simultaneously point me to God, who never fails to help.

When you are downhearted, discouraged or disappointed, the Psalms are a good place to turn for comfort. When you are battling with pain, death or loss, seek God as you read the Psalms. Set out below are some of the psalms you might turn to in times of trouble.

Psalm 34:1–9

I will extol the LORD at all times;
   his praise will always be on my lips.
My soul will boast in the LORD;
   let the afflicted hear and rejoice.
Glorify the LORD with me:
   let us exalt his name together.

I sought the LORD, and he answered me;
   he delivered me from all my fears.
Those who look to him are radiant;
   their faces are never covered with shame.
This poor man called, and the LORD heard him;
   he saved him out of all his troubles.
The angel of the LORD encamps around those who fear him,
   and he delivers them.

Taste and see that the LORD is good;
   blessed is the man who takes refuge in him.
Fear the LORD, you his saints,
   for those who fear him lack nothing.

Psalm 42

As the deer pants for streams of water,
   so my soul pants for you, O God.
My soul thirsts for God, for the living God.
   When can I go and meet with God?
My tears have been my food
   day and night,
while men say to me all day long,
   'Where is your God?'
These things I remember
   as I pour out my soul:

how I used to go with the multitude,
   leading the procession to the house of God,
with shouts of joy and thanksgiving
   among the festive throng.

Why are you downcast, O my soul?
   Why so disturbed within me?
Put your hope in God,
   for I will yet praise him,
   my Saviour and my God.

My soul is downcast within me;
   therefore I will remember you
from the land of the Jordan,
   the heights of Hermon – from Mount Mizar.
Deep calls to deep
   in the roar of your waterfalls;
all your waves and breakers
   have swept over me.

By day the LORD directs his love,
   at night his song is with me –
   a prayer to the God of my life.

I say to God my Rock,
   'Why have you forgotten me?
Why must I go about mourning,
   oppressed by the enemy?'
My bones suffer mortal agony
   as my foes taunt me,
saying to me all day long,
   'Where is your God?'

Why are you downcast, O my soul?
Why so disturbed within me?
Put your hope in God,
for I will yet praise him,
my Saviour and my God.

Psalm 55

Listen to my prayer, O God,
do not ignore my plea;
hear me and answer me.
My thoughts trouble me and I am distraught
at the voice of the enemy,
at the stares of the wicked;
for they bring down suffering upon me
and revile me in their anger.

My heart is in anguish within me;
the terrors of death assail me.
Fear and trembling have beset me;
horror has overwhelmed me.
I said, 'Oh, that I had the wings of a dove!
I would fly away and be at rest –
I would flee far away
and stay in the desert; *Selah*
I would hurry to my place of shelter,
far from the tempest and storm.'

Confuse the wicked, O Lord, confound their speech,
for I see violence and strife in the city.
Day and night they prowl about on its walls;
malice and abuse are within it.
Destructive forces are at work in the city;
threats and lies never leave its streets.

If an enemy were insulting me,
    I could endure it;
if a foe were raising himself against me,
    I could hide from him.
But it is you, a man like myself,
    my companion, my close friend,
with whom I once enjoyed sweet fellowship
    as we walked with the throng at the house of God.

Let death take my enemies by surprise;
    let them go down alive to the grave,
    for evil finds lodging among them.

But I call to God,
    and the LORD saves me.
Evening, morning and noon
    I cry out in distress,
    and he hears my voice.
He ransoms me unharmed
    from the battle waged against me,
    even though many oppose me.
God, who is enthroned for ever,
    will hear them and afflict them – *Selah*
men who never change their ways
    and have no fear of God.

My companion attacks his friends;
    he violates his covenant.
His speech is smooth as butter,
    yet war is in his heart;
his words are more soothing than oil,
    yet they are drawn swords.

Cast your cares on the LORD
    and he will sustain you;
    he will never let the righteous fall.
But you, O God, will bring down the wicked
    into the pit of corruption;
bloodthirsty and deceitful men
    will not live out half their days.

But as for me, I trust in you.

Psalm 73

Surely God is good to Israel,
    to those who are pure in heart.

But as for me, my feet had almost slipped;
    I had nearly lost my foothold.
For I envied the arrogant
    when I saw the prosperity of the wicked.

They have no struggles;
    their bodies are healthy and strong.
They are free from the burdens common to man;
    they are not plagued by human ills.
Therefore pride is their necklace;
    they clothe themselves with violence.
From their callous hearts comes iniquity;
    the evil conceits of their minds know no limits.
They scoff, and speak with malice;
    in their arrogance they threaten oppression.
Their mouths lay claim to heaven,
    and their tongues take possession of the earth.
Therefore their people turn to them
    and drink up waters in abundance.

They say, 'How can God know?
   Does the Most High have knowledge?'

This is what the wicked are like –
   always carefree, they increase in wealth.

Surely in vain have I kept my heart pure;
   in vain have I washed my hands in innocence.
All day long I have been plagued;
   I have been punished every morning.

If I had said, 'I will speak thus,'
   I would have betrayed your children.
When I tried to understand all this,
   it was oppressive to me
till I entered the sanctuary of God;
   then I understood their final destiny.

Surely you place them on slippery ground;
   you cast them down to ruin.
How suddenly are they destroyed,
   completely swept away by terrors!
As a dream when one awakes,
   so when you arise, O Lord,
   you will despise them as fantasies.

When my heart was grieved
   and my spirit embittered,
I was senseless and ignorant;
   I was a brute beast before you.

Yet I am always with you;
   you hold me by my right hand.

You guide me with your counsel,
    and afterwards you will take me into glory.
Whom have I in heaven but you?
    And earth has nothing I desire besides you.
My flesh and my heart may fail,
    but God is the strength of my heart
    and my portion for ever.

Those who are far from you will perish;
    you destroy all who are unfaithful to you.
But as for me, it is good to be near God.
    I have made the Sovereign LORD my refuge;
    I will tell of all your deeds.

Psalm 77

I cried out to God for help;
    I cried out to God to hear me.
When I was in distress, I sought the Lord;
    at night I stretched out untiring hands
    and my soul refused to be comforted.

I remembered you, O God, and I groaned;
    I mused, and my spirit grew faint. *Selah*
You kept my eyes from closing;
    I was too troubled to speak.
I thought about the former days,
    the years of long ago;
I remembered my songs in the night.
    My heart mused and my spirit enquired:

'Will the Lord reject for ever?
    Will he never show his favour again?
Has his unfailing love vanished for ever?

Has his promise failed for all time?
Has God forgotten to be merciful?
  Has he in anger withheld his compassion?' *Selah*

Then I thought, 'To this I will appeal:
  the years of the right hand of the Most High.'
I will remember the deeds of the LORD;
  yes, I will remember your miracles of long ago.
I will meditate on all your works
  and consider all your mighty deeds.

Your ways, O God, are holy.
  What god is so great as our God?
You are the God who performs miracles;
  you display your power among the peoples.
With your mighty arm you redeemed your people,
  the descendants of Jacob and Joseph. *Selah*

The waters saw you, O God,
  the waters saw you and writhed;
  the very depths were convulsed.
The clouds poured down water,
  the skies resounded with thunder;
  your arrows flashed back and forth.
Your thunder was heard in the whirlwind,
  your lightning lit up the world;
  the earth trembled and quaked.
Your path led through the sea,
  your way through the mighty waters,
  though your footprints were not seen.

You led your people like a flock
  by the hand of Moses and Aaron.

Psalm 84

How lovely is your dwelling-place,
    O Lord Almighty!
My soul yearns, even faints,
    for the courts of the Lord;
my heart and my flesh cry out
    for the living God.

Even the sparrow has found a home,
    and the swallow a nest for herself,
    where she may have her young –
a place near your altar,
    O Lord Almighty, my King and my God.
Blessed are those who dwell in your house;
    they are ever praising you. *Selah*

Blessed are those whose strength is in you,
    who have set their hearts on pilgrimage.
As they pass through the Valley of Baca,
    they make it a place of springs;
    the autumn rains also cover it with pools.
They go from strength to strength,
    till each appears before God in Zion.

Hear my prayer, O Lord God Almighty;
    listen to me, O God of Jacob. *Selah*
Look upon our shield, O God;
    look with favour on your anointed one.

Better is one day in your courts
    than a thousand elsewhere;
I would rather be a doorkeeper in the house of my God
    than dwell in the tents of the wicked.

For the LORD God is a sun and shield;
    the LORD bestows favour and honour;
no good thing does he withhold
    from those whose walk is blameless.

O LORD Almighty,
    blessed is the man who trusts in you.

Psalm 91

He who dwells in the shelter of the Most High
    will rest in the shadow of the Almighty.
I will say of the LORD, 'He is my refuge and my fortress,
    my God, in whom I trust.'

Surely he will save you from the fowler's snare
    and from the deadly pestilence.
He will cover you with his feathers,
    and under his wings you will find refuge;
    his faithfulness will be your shield and rampart.
You will not fear the terror of night,
    nor the arrow that flies by day,
nor the pestilence that stalks in the darkness,
    nor the plague that destroys at midday.
A thousand may fall at your side,
    ten thousand at your right hand,
    but it will not come near you.
You will only observe with your eyes
    and see the punishment of the wicked.

If you make the Most High your dwelling –
    even the LORD, who is my refuge –
then no harm will befall you,
    no disaster will come near your tent.

For he will command his angels concerning you
    to guard you in all your ways;
they will lift you up in their hands,
    so that you will not strike your foot against a stone.
You will tread upon the lion and the cobra;
    you will trample the great lion and the serpent.

'Because he loves me,' says the LORD, 'I will rescue him;
    I will protect him, for he acknowledges my name.
He will call upon me, and I will answer him;
    I will be with him in trouble,
    I will deliver him and honour him.
With long life will I satisfy him
    and show him my salvation.'

APPENDIX II: FURTHER READING

Carswell, Roger, *Comfort in Times of Sorrow* (Christian Focus, 2004)

Carswell, Roger, *Why Me?* (Authentic Media, 1993)

Dickson, John, *If I Were God I'd Stop All the Pain* (Good Book Company, 2001)

Dunn, Ronald, *When Heaven is Silent* (Word, 1994)

Elliot, Elizabeth, *These Strange Ashes* (OM Publishing, 1998)

Lewis, C. S., *A Grief Observed* (HarperCollins, 1961)

Lewis, C. S., *The Problem of Pain* (HarperCollins, 1940)

Wiersbe, Warren, *The Bumps Are What You Climb On: Encouragement for Difficult Days* (Baker Book House, 1982)

Wiersbe, Warren, *When Life Falls Apart* (Spire, 2001)

Wiersbe, Warren, *Why Us? When Bad Things Happen to God's People* (Fleming H. Revell Co., 1984)

NOTES

Chapter 1

1 Jean-Dominique Bauby, *The Diving-Bell and the Butterfly* (Fourth Estate, 1997).

2 Thornton Wilder, *The Bridge of San Luis Rey* (Penguin, 1927).

3 Deuteronomy 4:20; Job 23:10; Psalm 66:10; Isaiah 48:10; Jeremiah 6:29–30; 11:4; Ezekiel 22:18–22; Zechariah 13:8–9; Malachi 3:2–3; 1 Peter 1:6–7.

4 Job 9:17; 30:22; Psalm 42:7; 66:12; Jonah 2:3; Mark 4:39.

5 Job 16:14; 19:11–12; Lamentations 2:4–5; 1 Corinthians 16:13; 2 Timothy 2:3.

6 Jeremiah 4:31; Matthew 24:8; 1 Thessalonians 5:3.

7 Amos 9:9; Matthew 3:12; Luke 22:31.

8 Jeremiah 12:5.

9 Job 9:16, 29; 13:3.

10 Isaiah 55:8.

Chapter 2

1 Elie Wiesel, *Night* (Penguin, 1981).

2 Quote according to Lactantius in *A Treatise on the Anger of God*, cited in Warren Wiersbe, *Why Us?* (Fleming H. Revell Co., 1984).

3 Thomas Hardy, 'Nature's Questioning', *Everyman's Poetry: Thomas Hardy* (Everyman Paperbacks, 1998), p. 7.

4 Sir Alec Guinness, *Blessings in Disguise* (Penguin, 1985).

5 There is considerable evidence to substantiate the belief that the Bible is the word of God and Jesus the Son of God. The fulfilled prophecies of the Bible, as well as its unity in ideas, doctrines and even use of words, point to this collection of 66 books being inspired by one who is beyond time – knowing the past, present and future. The historical evidence of the resurrection of Jesus, three days after his crucifixion, provides every reason for believing that Jesus had power over death and was trustworthy in his claim to be God, doing what only God can do. See, for example, Josh McDowell, *Evidence that Demands a Verdict* (Campus Crusade for Christ, 1972).

6 Romans 11:33–34.

7 Psalm 89:14.

8 Revelation 15:3.

9 Deuteronomy 29:29.

10 Matthew Henry, *Zondervan NIV Matthew Henry Commentary* (Zondervan, 1992).

11 Penned by Dora Greenwell, 1821–82.

12 From a personal interview with the author.

13 Romans 8:28.

14 Warren Wiersbe, *Be Patient* (Kingsway, 1991).

15 Quote attributed to US essayist and poet Ralph Waldo Emerson (1803–82).

16 Habakkuk 3:17–18.

Chapter 3

1 John Milton, *Paradise Lost*, Book 8, lines 262–5.

2 Genesis 1:1.

3 Revelation 13:8.

4 Augustine of Hippo (AD 354–430).

5 Peter Balakian, *The Burning Tigris* (HarperCollins, 2003).

6 Ibid.

7 Ibid.

Chapter 4

1 Genesis 3 describes what happened.
2 Wladyslaw Szpilman, *The Pianist* (Phoenix, 1999).
3 *Daily Telegraph*, 14 January 2004.
4 Romans 3:23.
5 Matthew 22:37–39.
6 Matthew 7:11.
7 Taken from Charles Colson, *Who Speaks for God?* (Tyndale House, 1994).
8 Warren Wiersbe, *Why Us? When Bad Things Happen to God's People* (Fleming H. Revell Co., 1984).
9 John 9:1–3.
10 For example, Mark 7:20–23.

Chapter 5

1 John 1:1, 14.
2 Seven hundred years before Christ, Isaiah prophesied, 'For to us a child is born, to us a son is given, and the government will be on his shoulders. And he will be called Wonderful Counsellor, Mighty God, Everlasting Father, Prince of Peace. Of the increase of his government and peace there will be no end' (Isaiah 9:6–7). Even Jesus' birthplace was prophesied 500 years before his birth, by Micah: 'But you, Bethlehem Ephrathah, though you are small among the clans of Judah, out of you will come for me one who will be ruler over Israel, whose origins are from of old, from ancient times' (Micah 5:2). There are numerous other prophecies concerning the birth, life, death, rising again and influence of Jesus; for instance: Genesis 3:15; 21:12; 49:10; Isaiah 7:14; 8:14; 9:1–2; 35:5–6; 52:14; 53; Psalm 22.
3 Dorothy Sayers, *The Greatest Drama Ever Staged* (Hodder & Stoughton, 1938).
4 Mark 15:14.
5 Matthew 27:19.

6   Matthew 27:22.

7   Matthew 27:25.

8   Matthew 27:26.

9   For example, Matthew 20:18–19, 28; 21:42; John 10:17–18.

10 Galatians 1:4.

11 Titus 2:11–14.

12 *Daily Telegraph*, 19 December 2003.

13 Matthew 27:46.

14 2 Corinthians 5:21.

15 Luke 23:34.

16 Luke 23:46.

17 Quoted in Charles Colson, *Who Speaks for God?* (Tyndale, 1994).

18 1 John 1:7–9.

19 John 20:6–7.

20 This phrase is taken from a famous misquote of Bishop David Jenkins, previously Bishop of Durham 1984–94.

21 See, for instance, Professor Sir J. N. D. Anderson, *Christianity, the Witness of History* (Tyndale Press, 1970); Professor F. F. Bruce, *The New Testament Documents – Are They Reliable?* (IVP, 1959); or Roger Carswell, *Why Believe?* (Authentic Media, 1993).

22 John 14:6.

Chapter 6

1   Revelation 21:1–8.

2   Rodney Hartman, *Ali: The Life of Ali Bacher* (Penguin, 2004).

3   Romans 6:23.

4   Matthew 23:37.

5   Revelation 20:11–15.

6   The martyrdom of St Polycarp, Bishop of Smyrna, was recorded in the letter of the Church of Smyrna to the Church of Philomelium: see *Apostolic Fathers, Ante-Nicene Library* (T. & T. Clark).

7   Psalm 73:25.
8   Psalm 73:28.

Chapter 7

1   Leo Tolstoy, *A Confession and What I Believe* (Oxford University Press, 1921).
2   2 Corinthians 5:17.
3   Ken Abraham and Lisa Beamer, *Let's Roll!* (Tyndale House, 2005).
4   Revelation 21:3–4.

Chapter 8

1   1 Peter 5:7.
2   Luke 24:32.
3   Luke 24:46–47.
4   1 Thessalonians 4:13.
5   Psalm 42:5.
6   Psalm 42:8.
7   Acts 16:25.
8   The Spafford story, and the hymn in its original version, can be found at <http://www.spafford-kids.org/history_mission.htm>.
9   John 11:25–26.
10 John 11:25–26.
11 Deuteronomy 31:8.

Chapter 9

1   C. S. Lewis, *Mere Christianity* (HarperCollins, 1952).
2   This story can be found in Matthew 18:21–35.
3   Her story is told in *Journey to Murder – Road to Forgiveness* by Jo Pollard (Authentic Media, 2001).
4   Matthew 5:7.
5   Luke 11:4.
6   Luke 23:34.
7   Ephesians 4:32.

8   Genesis 50:20.

9   Romans 12:21.

10   Galatians 4:4.

Chapter 10

1   Statistic taken from the United Nations site
    <http://www.unstats.un.org/unsd/mi/mi_worldregn.asp>.

2   Story told by Lindsay Brown, General Secretary of IFES, at the
    IFES Europe & Eurasia 'Get Connected' conference in
    Hungary, Easter 2004.

3   Micah 6:8.

4   Mark 6:34.

5   1 John 3:17–18.

6   Luke 4:18, where Jesus is quoting from Isaiah 61:1–2.

7   Nelson Mandela, *Long Walk to Freedom* (Little, Brown & Co.,
    1995).

8   Psalm 42:5–6.

9   In the prophecy in Isaiah 53:3.

10   Isaiah 45:3.

Chapter 11

1   <http://www.janisian.com/lyrics>. 'At Seventeen', words and
    music by Janis Ian © 1974. Reproduced by permission of EMI
    Music Publishing Japan Ltd/EMI Music Publishing Ltd, London
    WC2H OHY.

2   Matthew 6:25–34.

3   Psalm 55:22.

4   In a letter dated 29 April 1959.

5   Isaiah 40:28–31.

6   John 13:7.

7   From a talk entitled 'When you get to the end of your rope',
    delivered at the Association of Evangelists Conference, England,
    November 2000.

8 Acts 10:38.

9 3 John 2.

10 Romans 8:28.

11 Jeremiah 29:13.

12 Revelation 21:6.

13 Revelation 21:4.

14 Matthew 11:28.

Conclusion

1 Luke 13:1–5.

2 John 9:3.

3 The full story is found in *Why Me?* by Roger Carswell (Authentic Media, 1993).

4 I quoted this story in a booklet called *Disaster*, which I published after the Hillsborough tragedy in 1989, but sadly I have no further source details.

5 Matthew 11:28.

6 2 Corinthians 5:19.

7 Acts 2:21, quoting Joel 2:32.

PABLO MARTINEZ

A
THORN in the
Flesh

FINDING STRENGTH AND
HOPE AMID SUFFERING

'If there *is* a God of love, why is there so much suffering in the world?' Pablo Martinez, with his personal experience of 'thorns', does not give glib answers but provides a well-balanced, well-researched and biblical commentary on suffering of all kinds.

He deals in detail with the thorns Paul endured throughout his life as a follower of Christ and explains these thorns as loss – whether of health, limb, freedom or a loved one – and explores the resultant emotions, such as anger, depression and anxiety. The necessity, he says, is to deal with these emotions, rather than nurture them: *'the way in which we face our own thorns in life is the best sermon that we can ever preach.'*

A Thorn in the Flesh will prove to be a very useful resource for those suffering from their own thorns as well as for those aiming to give help and comfort.

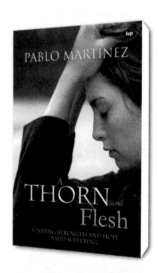

ISBN:
978-1-84474-188-5

Available from your local Christian bookshop or via our website at **www.ivpbooks.com**

related titles

Beyond the Edge

Hazel Rolston

One woman's journey out of
post-natal depression and anxiety

'Broken, desperate and humiliated, I entered the house. When I saw Steve and Katherine, my heart felt like it was going to explode in agony. They did not deserve this madness in their lives ...'

Cut off by a dense fog of post-natal depression and anxiety, Hazel Rolston felt pushed beyond the edge. But when the grim voice of Despair offered her the path of suicide, she knew instinctively that this was not God's way for her.

Hazel doesn't offer us a formula for instant escape. But she does remind us that God is there, even if our feelings say the opposite. No matter how bad things feel, God is faithful to his wounded, broken people beyond the edge.

'Read this book and be changed to reach out with Jesus' compassion.'
Alie Stibbe

'As Hazel lays bare her heart, we discover, not slogans or rhetoric, but authentic hope. This gritty, immensely readable book is more than a tonic. It's a lifesaver.'
Jeff Lucas

ISBN:
978-1-84474-216-5

Available from your local Christian bookshop or via our website at www.ivpbooks.com

www.ivpbooks.com

For more details of books published by IVP, visit our website where you will find all the latest information, including:

Book extracts	Downloads
Author interviews	Online bookshop
Reviews	Christian bookshop finder

You can also sign up for our regular email newsletters, which are tailored to your particular interests, and tell others what you think about this book by posting a review.

We publish a wide range of books on various subjects including:

Christian living	Small-group resources
Key reference works	Topical issues
Bible commentary series	Theological studies